If They Can Sell Pet Rocks Why Can't You Sell Your Business

(FOR WHAT YOU WANT)?

John Martinka

ISBN: 1495478254
ISBN 13: 9781495478253
Library of Congress Control Number: 2014902873
CreateSpace Independent Publishing Platform
North Charleston, South Carolina

Contents

Acknowledgments

Thanks to my wife, Jan, for tolerating the intensity of my moving from the writing and publishing of *Buying a Business That Makes You Rich—Toss Your Job Not the Dice* right into writing this book, all when my consulting business was very busy.

Also to my wonderful sons, daughters, their spouses and our grand-kids, and my mother-in-law who was so excited to say her son-in-law is an author (after the first book).

A special thanks to Alan Weiss, my mentor and coach over the last 15 years, who convinced me to share my expertise by writing books and whose idea it was for the title of this book.

Finally, I'd like to thank two good friends, Dobre and Rocket. Dobre is our lab flat-coated retriever and Rocket is our rat terrier. We have a lot of fun together.

Preface

Pet Rock

From *Wikipedia*: "Pet Rocks were a 1970s collectible conceived by advertising executive Gary Dahl. The first Pet Rocks were ordinary gray stones bought at a builder's supply store. They were marketed like live pets, in custom cardboard boxes, complete with straw and breathing holes for the "animal." The fad lasted about six months, ending after a short increase in sales during the Christmas season of December 1975. Although by February 1976 they were discounted due to lower sales, Dahl sold 1.5 million Pet Rocks and became a millionaire."

Business for Sale

One of millions of companies (annually) that the owner wants sell. Unfortunately, perhaps as few as 20% of these companies ever sell. With an aging population of business owners (2014 studies show that over 50% of all owners are over the age of 50) it's vitally important owners position their business to be one of the companies that sell and sell for full value.

Business Buyer

A skeptical by nature person, whether buying individually or on behalf of a company, who discounts anything good they hear about a business and always fears there are questions they are not asking correctly or for which they are not getting the complete answer. When they uncover even one small item they feel was "not disclosed properly" it casts doubt on all other information they've received about the business.

Introduction

While researching this book, I discovered that there are very few books that discuss making a company more attractive to a buyer. Most books in this genre have to do with the actual selling process, legal contracts, negotiations, and similar. Typically these books devoted only 10 to 25 percent of the text to the subject of making the business more attractive to buyers; those on the higher end of the scale were books aimed at the middle market and private equity targets ($25 million or more in sales). Yet over 95 percent of companies in the United States have fewer than fifty employees.

This led me to devote 90 percent of this book to the strategies needed to make your business more appealing to buyers. After working with hundreds of buyers and sellers and completing over one hundred transactions, I've noted what scares buyers and what attracts them, what questions they will ask (or should ask) and what will enthrall them. In chapter nine you'll learn the most important thing you can say to a buyer.

What really excites buyers is seeing where they can add value and feeling they can take the business to the next level (with their skills, knowledge, and experience). Imagine your business is like a server rack. Server racks typically have numerous slots filled with servers and some empty slots. If buyers see your business as one where they can fill the same slots (each server representing the talents and value you bring to your company) they might be interested. If they doubt they can fill all the slots you do, they will likely not be interested. However, if they believe they and your management team can fill all of your slots plus an empty slot or two (with the increased value they bring to the business), they will be motivated and excited.

This doesn't mean buyers want to see a lot of dysfunctional areas in the business (although if they do see dysfunction, they may also see opportunity, albeit at a lower price). "Adding value" means that the buyer believes he brings something to build on what is already there. Here are three examples:

1. The seller of a contract manufacturing business did no aerospace work. The buying group had extensive aerospace experience and contacts. They saw a company with a base of business on which they could expand the customer base, which was how they could add value.

2. A buyer saw a company that was doing very well but had reached the limits of the owner's management abilities. The buyer had the leadership, management, and organizational skills to take what the seller had built and expand it, another way of adding value.

3. The seller's marketing was stale and outdated, and the website was nothing more than a brochure. Within two months the buyer converted the website to a platform to order and book the firm's services. This saved customers' and staff time, and productivity increased tremendously—allowing the business to double in size in two years.

The following graphic is one I use when presenting to business owners. All businesses are somewhere on the line from start-up to legacy. When entrepreneurs start a business they are doers. They have to make the product, write the code, cook the food, deliver the service, and so on. At some point, many of them (not all) become managers (where others do the work) and leaders (true CEOs), and a select few leave a legacy, whether it's the company name, their name, or business continuation to future generations.

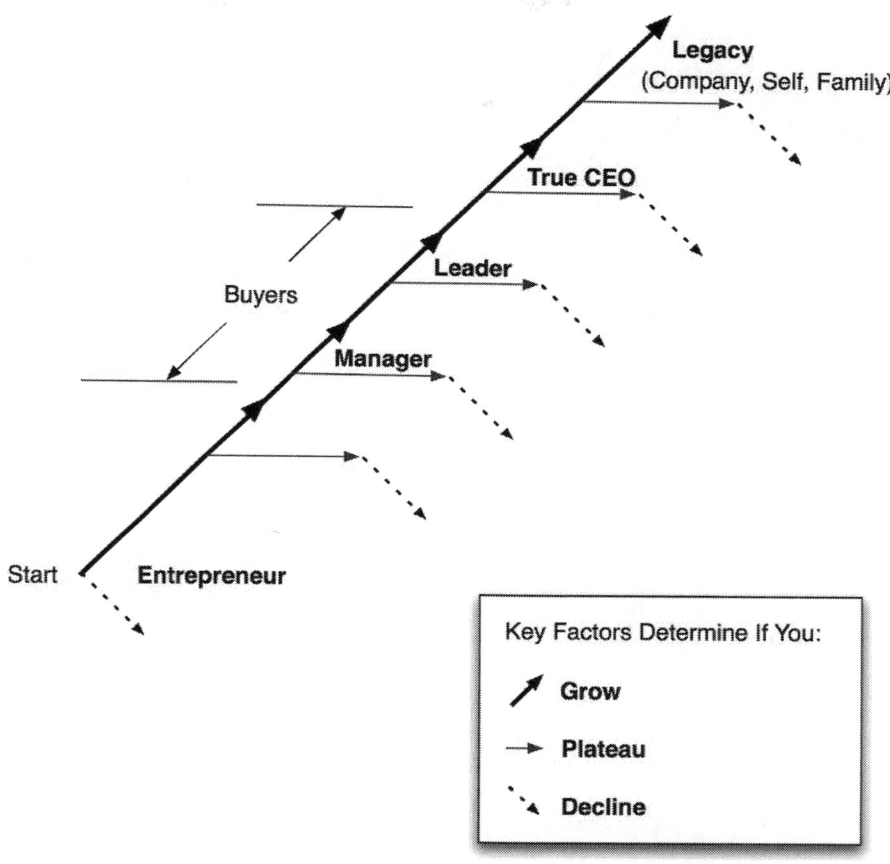

Business buyers will generally want something from the manager level up. Knowing where you are on the scale, coupled with other factors, allows you to determine who your logical buyer is. For example, a private equity group is probably not going to be interested in a business, no matter what the size, if the owner is nothing more than a doer with some management skills. Private equity wants to see management depth.

Individual buyers will start to fade out of the picture as the business gets to the point where the owner is a true CEO. A company with a full management team and an owner who works only on the big picture is probably going to be better for a strategic buyer (another company), private equity, or an investment group.

Understanding this puts you in a better position to prepare your company correctly so you can exit with style, grace, and more money.

Chapter One

An ACTION™ plan to sell your business

"Nobody is going to buy your business" is a statement that can deflate an owner just as sure as a pin to a balloon will send it spinning around the room.

George's CPA referred him to me when he was interested in selling the business he had started a decade earlier. We had a thorough discussion about the business, and I reviewed five years' of the company's financial statements and tax returns. It was at this point that I made the above statement.

The company's sales and profits had been on a rollercoaster ride. Six-figure losses one year and six-figure profits the next, although never enough to recoup previous losses. There were large negative retained earnings and substantial bank debt, and accounts payable were in excess of cash and accounts receivables.

George had an outside interest, and when business was good, he got very involved with his other interest until business became bad, and he was forced to return to managing the company. The wide swings in revenues and profits were because George was the primary salesperson for the company, so when he wasn't working sales declined. In other words, the business had a huge dependency, and it was George.

This wasn't the only problem with the business. George had hired his romantic interest, paying her an executive salary for doing administrative work and running errands. There was no business plan, no marketing plan, and no budgeting. Actually there was no planning of any kind; everything was done on the fly. It didn't take very long to figure out what we needed to do: planning, budgeting, and monitoring.

Our first meeting was about July 1, a very, very slow time for George's industry. Within a few weeks we had a sales and marketing strategy outlined and in place. I insisted they monitor every activity related to sales: marketing letters, telephone calls, in-person sales calls, proposals, and so on. For the six weeks before Labor Day, the company turned into a marketing machine, instead of just coasting through the summer as they usually did. Their last six months of that year ended with sales 33 percent above their forecast, and that momentum continued into the next year.

By the next summer, George was entertaining interest from two industry buyers and one outside buyer. He received an offer, but turned it down. With some systems in place, momentum and consistent profits convinced him he didn't have to sell. He continued to operate and grow the business, making small improvements along the way. Five years later he sold to a competitor for substantially more than the previous offers. In fact, the down payment was significantly higher than the full price he was originally offered.

George had become a prisoner of (and in) his business. We created an escape plan after it became evident to him that his business was not salable. The purpose of this book is to help you create your escape plan well in advance so you control the escape and its timing.

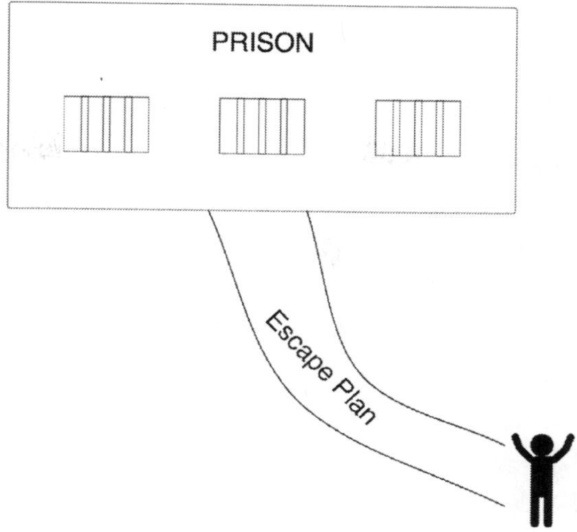

Exiting with style, grace, and more money all sound good, but the fact is, very few owners do any preparation.

The difference between home sellers and business sellers

Take the following to heart:

Business sellers could learn a lot from home sellers.

I used to believe that the biggest difference between the two was that while home sellers invite the world in to see what's for sale, business sellers demand the utmost in confidentiality. I now realize that the *biggest difference* is that home sellers prepare the heck out of the house and business owners do next to nothing to show the business in its best light.

The more you prepare, the lower the odds of seller remorse. When you prepare, you'll realize one of two things:

1. You are fully committed to selling.

2. You really aren't ready and will keep running your improved business.

Either way, you win and potential buyers win.

Baby boomers are your threat to a higher price

What are your odds?

Since 2010 a huge generational shift has been taking place. In 2008 the first "baby boomer" (born 1946) started collecting Social Security at age sixty-two. At the same time, the US government has delayed "full" Social Security retirement benefits until age seventy. Estimates are that ten thousand people a day become eligible for Medicare; this will continue for almost two decades.

That is a lot of people reaching what has traditionally been retirement age. While it has economists, budget analysts, and the like scared because of the drain on our unfunded or underfunded Social Security system, *it should make business sellers sweat and buyers jump for joy.* This generation has always been entrepreneurial. In fact, according to Intuit, as of 2009, people between the ages of fifty-five and sixty-four accounted for the highest percentage of any ten-year age group starting businesses. As said in the Preface, over half of all business owners are age fifty and over.

In 2008 *The Wall Street Journal*, in an article titled, "Want to Sell a Business? You May Not Be Ready," by Arden Dale, predicted that from 2008 to 2018, 70 percent of medium-sized businesses will change hands ("medium-sized" was not defined). The article also stated that 90 percent of these businesses are "ill prepared" for a sale.

This is what business buyers like to hear, as it often means there is potential to improve the current operation and immediately increase profits. In 2011 PriceWaterhouseCoopers predicted that two-thirds of companies with $5 to 50 million in sales would change hands in the next ten years. Due to the Great Recession, this ten-year period keeps getting pushed out. That's because of what's in a 2010 SunTrust Bank survey: 43 percent of business owners were delaying their exit by at least two years because of the recession. In 2013 that bubble started to appear.

No matter what the actual numbers are, there will be a high percentage of small to midsized privately held companies on the market in the next decade. There are twenty to twenty-five million fewer people in the generation behind the baby-boomer generation (generation X). And, according to the Intuit study mentioned above, this generation is not as entrepreneurial as the baby-boomer generation and, therefore, owners without an exit strategy will likely sell at a discount if they can't find the right buyer if there's a shortage of buyers.

The numbers show that generation Y, following generation X, is approximately the same size as the baby-boomer generation. According to the Intuit study, this generation is incredibly entrepreneurial. In fact, the study states, "Generation Y [is] the most entrepreneurial generation ever."

The last statement is not good news for sellers. Even though on first glance one would think it is good news for retiring business owners. However, business buyers are trading capital for cash flow. They make a down payment, some or all from personal funds, and walk into a salary and profits (used to pay the acquisition debt). However, this younger generation doesn't have the experience to convince most owners to sell their business and finance part of the sale. Plus, they usually won't have the capital for either a down payment or an all-cash transaction.

To summarize, the odds are against owners whose businesses are unprepared for sale. Owners who take the time to prepare for the eventual sale of their business, whether it's in months or years, will maximize their return. Those who aren't prepared will always think their business was worth more than it sold for and wonder why they couldn't get a higher price.

Why should and why do owners sell?

Let's address the main reasons, not the exceptions. First we need to eliminate all the owners who are selling because they are losing money. Buying a loser usually involves special circumstances, which we'll look at in chapter two.

To a buyer, the more catastrophic the event (affecting the owner, not the business) the more urgency there is to sell. Buyers look for the three Ds:

- Divorce
- Death
- Disability

These things really happen. A buyer recently closed a deal for a business sold by the widower of the deceased owner. After a long illness, the owner died and the spouse had been "holding it together" for a couple years. He told the buyer he was the only one allowed to sign checks, and he did that so the employees would think he was paying attention to the business. As a seller, this is not a situation you, or your family, want to be in.

Most deals happen in the following circumstances:

1. The owner is burned out.
2. The owner or spouse has health issues arise.
3. The owner has sufficient management abilities for the business's current size.
4. The owner has other ideas to pursue (the entrepreneurial spirit).

5. Retirement beckons.

6. Life happens (personal events force a sale).

On a scale of one to ten, with ten being "I wish I had sold yesterday" and one being "Pay me four times what it's worth, all in cash, and I'll sell," these people are a seven, eight, or nine. Sometimes owners at a six or even a five can be influenced to sell when the right buyer shows up. They realize it's better to sell now to the right person than to wait and either not find the right buyer or have a tumultuous selling experience trying to find the right buyer.

Ideally the seller would be able to say, "The reason for the sale is that it is part of the exit planning process I began three years ago." As with the example of George, if that exit planning is documented, step by step, it not only builds a case that, yes, it is true the seller planned for a sale after three to five years of preparation, but it also shows that all the steps taken as part of the preparation process had a positive effect on the business. And, if those actions didn't have a positive effect, the buyer won't have to waste time and money experimenting in that area.

Real-Life Story

Often I talk to owners (sellers) who tell me they don't work too hard, they are coasting, and so on. They speak of this as a positive, but it isn't always a positive. Keith bought a company that was truly coasting. The owner was seventy and sales had peaked when he was sixty-five. One thing that attracted Keith to the business was he saw that the owner took numerous vacations of up to four weeks every year. He knew that just by his being there the business would do better; and it did after he bought it.

Scott, on the other hand, discounted the value of a company he really wanted to buy because it was evident that not only was the owner coasting, but also there was a culture of not working hard in the firm, a culture of working just enough to make the level of income the owner and salespeople wanted. Scott realized there would be resistance to the energy and drive he would bring to the company. It was an aging employee base; it's a lot easier when the employee base is younger, as was the case with Keith's company.

Sellers, realize that business buyers are a skeptical lot. And this skepticism comes with good reason. All you have to do is peruse the Internet business buy-sell sites to see all the pitches and how often the word *potential* is used. A buyer wants to see that the profile summary of the business, the financial statements, and the tax returns at least look like they are from the same company.

It's your life, so give it serious consideration

Let's assume you are selling for reasons other than a catastrophic event. You may be retiring, getting burned out, or just ready to seek your next great adventure in life. You must pay attention to the "softer" issues. They are much more important than the hard facts of having an exit plan or actually selling your business. These are things that aren't usually involved in a forced sale (the three Ds).

Are you ready?

Selling your business is often an emotional rollercoaster. Don't ignore this or it will hit you upside the head like a linebacker at full speed spearing a wide receiver. A large part of this book deals with getting your business ready for sale, but the eight-hundred-pound gorilla in the room is the question, "Are *you* ready to sell?" Seller remorse hits when you realize you got caught up in the moment and can't fathom not going in to the business (your baby) every day. If you're coasting because you can't bear the thought of leaving, realize:

Value decreases as the owner gets burned out.

I tell business buyers to approach an acquisition with the understanding that it's a five- to ten-year engagement and investment. If you end up falling in love with it, great. But don't look for the perfect business you'll be married to forever. Understand that at some time you will leave the business, and it's your decision if you leave by dying at your desk at age ninety or selling when the time is right.

I am often asked how I handle my clients' emotional issues when involved in buy-sell transactions. I do a lot of handholding as we glide through this life-changing event and the largest financial transaction in their lives, much larger than the value of their home. It's important to take time to think and talk through these issues. There is no right or wrong; just make the effort to understand and deal with it so you make the right decision for your family and you.

Whose decision is it really?

If the big question is "Are you ready to sell?" then an even bigger question might be "Is your spouse ready to sell?"

During one of my annual Getting the Deal Done breakfast conferences, our panel was asked about decision-making and decision makers on buy-sell transactions of all sizes. My answer was, "In consulting with large companies, it is very important to find and deal with the true buyer, the person who can say yes without asking anybody else for approval. In the buying and selling of family-owned businesses, the true buyer is often the spouse."

Owners have told me their spouse wants to travel before they are too old, they want to move near their kids and grandkids that have moved away, or their spouse has health issues that the owner must deal with. On the flip side, I've known owners whose spouse was against selling for reasons of income or having to be together all the time.

Real-Life Story

My client was two months or more into the selling process. He'd had a valuation done on the business; we had packaged information about the company and had an outline of an offer. He then said, "I guess I better talk to my wife about this." Boom! The process came to a screeching halt, and his wife felt betrayed that he hadn't discussed selling with her. (The buyer and I both had heard from the seller that all was OK with his wife regarding selling.)

Once she calmed down, her next issue was that she didn't want him around the house all the time. That issue was (somewhat) solved when he reminded her that he hadn't been going in to the business every day for quite a while, and with a new general manager on board he would be around more than ever. ("So get used to it, honey.")

No matter what the size of your company, no matter what your age or situation—consult with your spouse first, and make him or her part of the process.

What do you need (financially)?

Your financial planner is a valuable member of your team. Know what you need financially. If you're retiring, do you need money from the sale to supplement your other assets and income? Do you need enough money to buy or start another business?

In any event, work with your investment advisor so you have a clear picture. The only thing worse than finding out during the selling process that the proceeds aren't enough for what you want to do is finding out postsale that you are short funds.

Tips:

- *Don't* get income projections from somebody whose goal is to sell you products or services. This could be insurance, investments, or money management. It's better to pay a fee for impartial advice than to get a glamorous but erroneous report.

- *Do* get detailed projections including the probability of your assets lasting well past your spouse's and your life expectancy based on various investment strategies.

And remember, projections are nothing but estimates based on a series of assumptions. They are not a guarantee and need to be monitored. Evaluating your personal situation well in advance allows you to get a business valuation and prepare the business to meet your financial requirements.

What will you do?

The previous Real-Life Story showcases the spousal tension issue, which is quite common. My aunt and uncle owned and ran a sporting goods and hardware store for decades, but they are the exception. Most people can't work with their spouse and shouldn't be together 24/7 after selling their business.

The seller who has a plan of varied activities postsale comes across as a lot more serious about selling compared to the owner who has no plan. Take some time to think about this, discuss it with family, and know what you're going to do. There used to be a story (true or not, I don't know) about all the Boeing people who died at age sixty-seven or sixty-eight because their life had changed so dramatically. Social Security was designed with a retirement age of sixty-five because in the 1930s life expectancy for men at sixty-five was about sixty-eight.

Don't let your business be your life. It should be a component of your life that gives your life meaning and provides you with a lifestyle.

Those you love (and like)

Do you care about your children and employees and what will happen to them post-sale? If one or more of your children are active in the business, you need to decide what happens to them if you sell to an outside buyer. You might want to consider selling to your children. It can't be a sentimental decision; your children must be qualified to run the business and pay you for it.

Real-Life Story

A business owner died and his son, the shop foreman, inherited the business. He was not capable of running the business, and over the next two years it declined to the point that it was unsalable.

If you want your children to have the skills to run the business, then groom them on the management of the firm; don't wait until it's too late.

Another owner told me he was upset because neither his son nor his daughter wanted to take over his business. I asked what his children did and he replied that one was a lawyer and the other was a doctor. You'd think he'd be proud, not disappointed.

The same goes for your loyal employees, especially your management. Do they have the guts to buy the business? Do they have the money? Are they willing to sign a personal guarantee and put up personal collateral to the bank?

One final word on this: work with your attorney, family, and life insurance agent in advance if you have one or more children active in the business and one or more not active in the business. It can be done, but it takes planning to make sure all are treated fairly. Those active in the business won't want to work hard to have dividends go to their siblings, and those not active will feel slighted if you favor those children working in the business (especially if the business is the vast majority of your net worth).

Who is your potential buyer?

There are two classes of business buyers, strategic and financial. Within those classes there are seven types of business buyer; although each type has its unique features, there is some overlap:

1. Individuals (or partners)
2. Search funds
3. Family and/or management team
4. Small business owners (growth by acquisition)
5. Large companies (strategic buyers)
6. Private equity groups
7. Family offices and fundless sponsors

Financial buyers

A business buyer is a business buyer, right? Wrong. There are different types of buyers, with different criteria and objectives. Most business buyers are financial buyers; there are also strategic buyers and private equity group (PEG) buyers of varying sizes and with varying objectives.

All buyers want financial rewards. The term "financial buyer" refers to those who are in need of immediate and constant financial rewards. On the other end, strategic buyers have the ability to delay financial rewards.

Individuals—Financial buyers are usually individuals, often corporate refugees who want to escape the corporate world. They have often dreamed of business ownership for years and view a job loss as the stimulus they need to make the leap to entrepreneurship. You may have been a corporate refugee at one time.

They have honed their management (and other) skills and built their capital in the corporate world. Buying a business is usually the best option for them given their age, career position, and lack of creativity or that they have no idea for a new business. Creators start businesses; managers and leaders take the idea to the next level.

Financial buyers are looking for, first of all, a mature, profitable company. They want the business to be fairly priced as their needs include the following:

- A fair-market salary for the job of company president
- Scalability—most buyers want a business they can work *on* versus work *in*
- Profits in addition to salary—this is how the buyer will pay off acquisition debt, fund growth, and cover any hiccups to the business
- Not only income, but also net-worth increase (like you have achieved through business ownership)—every payment they make on the acquisition debt increases their personal net worth because those payments come from the profit the business generates
- A deal structure that allows them to make a down payment from their personal funds (including the help of friends and family) with the rest of the price covered by a bank loan and/or seller financing

- A business that is salable in the future—something they feel can be grown, in an industry that has a future and is attractive to buyers or where growth can lead to a sale to a corporate buyer or private equity group

- Manageable risk—people who buy businesses are usually more risk-averse than people who start businesses (my friend Bill Pearsall, a Bellevue, WA, business broker, calls buyers "re-entrepreneurs," a very apropos term)

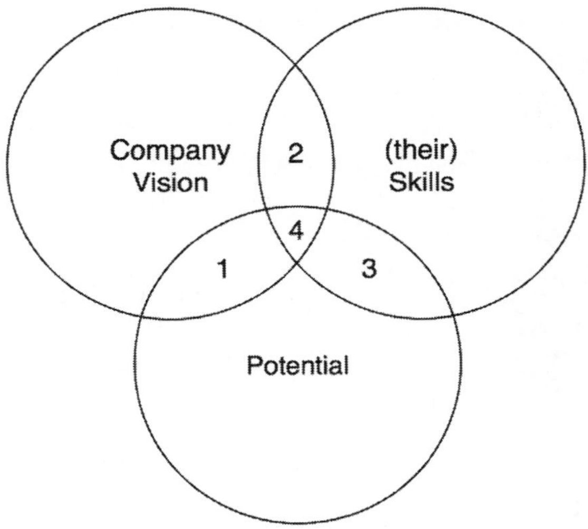

The above diagram shows the following:

1. A company with vision and potential will fail if the buyer doesn't have the right skills.

2. If the buyer has the skills and the business has vision (strategy), but the business has no potential, it will stagnate.

3. Skills and potential without a vision means the buyer will be lost, chasing too much and achieving little.

4. When all three elements are present, the sale, transition, and future of the company will likely be successful.

Real-Life Story

I also work with business buyers as a Business Buyer Advocate. I help my clients hone their value propositions for sellers and their businesses. Often this means getting them to reduce the number of filters they have for what makes a good acquisition candidate.

Here's an example that I framed for a client after observing him, what he liked, what he didn't like, and so on. I told him, "You need a business where you can create or expand business-to-business sales channels, probably for a service and with steady, recurring work."

If your business requires a manufacturing-process expert as the owner, this buyer's not for you. On the other hand, if your business is sales and relationship driven, it's not going to be good for a manufacturing engineer.

I tell you the above story so you can screen buyers properly. Besides the right skills for your business, what else does a buyer need to have to be a fit for you? First, you won't sell to someone you don't like. If you don't have the same business philosophy, don't trust the person, or have any other reasons not to do a deal or build a relationship, walk away.

Second, the right buyer has to have enough money to do the deal. It's one of the legs of the stool that makes someone a qualified business buyer.

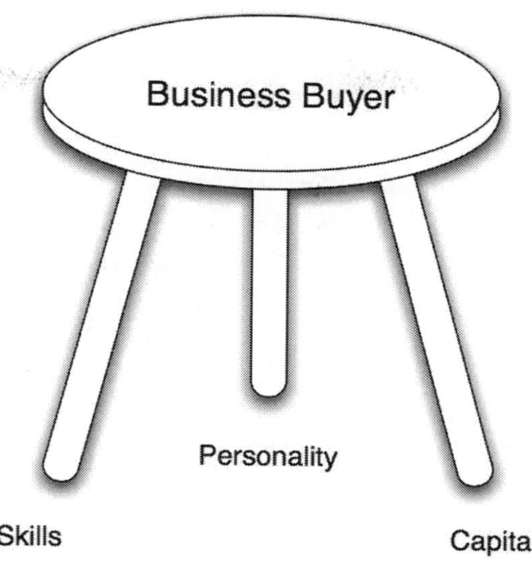

Now, you have a very similar three-legged stool. While the buyer needs capital, you need to have profits. While she needs to have the right skills, you need to have systems and market potential for growth. You both need to have a good personality so you can build a relationship.

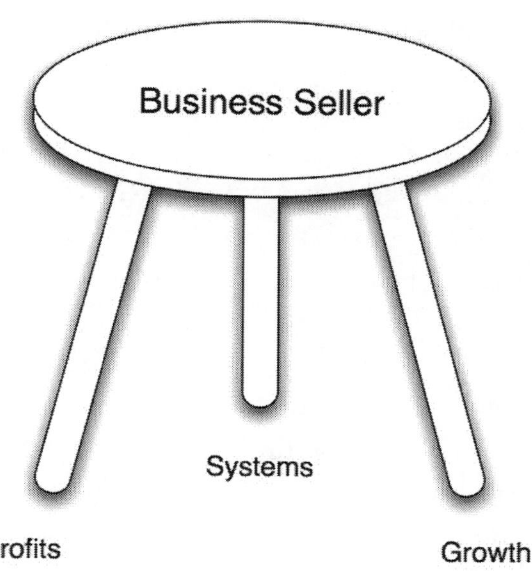

Private equity groups and related platform companies— A private equity group (PEG) raises funds from investors to invest in companies, typically companies with $5 million or more of EBITDA (earnings before interest, taxes, depreciation, and amortization). Their focus varies from group to group, as does their holding period. Some want to buy and hold for the medium or long term, while others want to turn companies every five to seven years to return money to their investors. Over the years there's been a blending of venture capital (VC) firms and PEGs as the market for VC deals has shrunk.

Search fund buyers—Search fund buyers are a hybrid of individual buyers and PEGs. They want a larger business than they can afford on their own, so they raise money to fund a search (i.e., pay themselves while searching) and the investors get first right of refusal to invest in deals based on how much they funded the search. The investors could be high-net-worth individuals, hedge funds, PEGs, or others. The buyer is trading 100 percent ownership on a smaller business for minority ownership (about 20 percent with increased equity based on performance) in a much larger company. Search fund buyers also have to pay attention to their investors' likes and dislikes when it comes to business types and when the investors want their money returned.

Small business owners—In chapter two we discuss growing by acquisition as a strategy. This approach, implemented by another business, could be your best exit strategy. Keep in mind that selling to a direct competitor is one of the most sensitive things you can do. Be careful!

Large companies—Selling to another business is often referred to as selling to a strategic buyer, and the larger the company the more strategic it becomes. One of my clients previously worked for a large firm that averaged two acquisitions a year. He told me that they looked for a product, a market, and engineers. They could provide sales, marketing, systems, and the other things needed to maximize return on investment. This made them ideal buyers for product-driven companies that hadn't figured out the marketing piece. Can larger companies pay more? Yes, if you meet their size and scope criteria and they can justify the ROI.

Real-Life Story

A friend was selling his business that did about $20 million in annual sales and was quite profitable. He told me there were three potential buyers, including one strategic buyer and one pure financial buyer. The financial buyer made the best offer!

Just because a company is seen as a strategic buyer doesn't mean it will automatically pay more. As I write this, I'm involved in negotiations for a large industry player to buy a "small" business in the same industry. The buyer's starting point for pricing is the value of the assets. Like with my friend's situation, they're just not throwing money around.

Family and/or management—Selling to family or management is sometimes an option, if they're willing to take the risk. Often you'll get a higher price but less cash. Banks like the fact that these potential buyers have industry and company experience. Unfortunately, too often these buyers expect a gift, whether it's a low price, favorable terms, or not having to guarantee their loan.

According to *The Kiplinger Letter*, 15 percent of family-owned businesses make it to the third generation. However, I get looks of skepticism as most owners and advisors think that figure is high. No matter what the figure, it is not an everyday occurrence to sell a business to a family member (or management team).

Real-Life Story

I helped two owners transition the business to their son. We set a benchmark of what the business was worth, they worked on growth strategies for a number of years, and we then revisited the value of the business.

Along the way they hired their son as a salesperson; he did so well he became the sales manager. They gifted him with 10 percent of the stock and mentored him as he worked his way up the ladder to be the company president (Dad was CEO and Mom CFO).

Mom and Dad worked their way out of the day-to-day operations and concentrated on strategy and vision. They were able to take month-long vacations (to test that their son and the team were ready). The eventual transition for the other 90 percent of the stock was no cash down and a twenty-year payment plan (their retirement annuity).

When selling to family members or management, realize there is a good chance there will be a smaller down payment and, therefore, more generous terms with a longer payout period. To compensate, the price will usually be higher than if a buyer with cash makes a significant down payment. However, the management team or family has a greater chance of success if they have been active in the company's management for years.

Included in this category are ESOPs (employee stock ownership plans). There are estimated to be between eleven and twelve thousand of this type of qualified retirement plan currently active in the United States (out of about twenty million businesses). There are tax and borrowing advantages to ESOPs, and usually all full-time employees with the minimum required tenure own part of the company through this plan. They are not inexpensive to set up, have to follow ERISA and, as in selling to management or family, there has to be some leadership in the employee group. If interested in an ESOP, I recommend you consult with an expert in the field. This is a lot more complicated than simply selling to a third-party buyer.

Real-Life Story

Matthew bought his company after the management team wouldn't personally guarantee loans or pledge collateral to the bank. The thought of owning the business excited the management team, but the thought of signing a note with the bank, pledging their homes as collateral, and signing a note with the seller scared them out of the deal. The bank had approved the loan with a very small down payment because they were the ideal buyers, being the management team for the firm.

They wanted a risk-free deal, or maybe they thought it would be a guaranteed job without any financial responsibility. Matthew walked into a great situation and a very loyal and dedicated team. A side benefit of a management team passing on a deal is that you know they will not be going out to start or buy a business and become your competitor.

On the flip side, they have proven not to be Matthew's exit strategy.

Family offices and fundless sponsors—The "family office" is a fairly recent phenomenon in which very-wealthy people have their complete financial life run by a family office management firm. The firm handles everything from investments to paying the monthly bills. In recent years the investment side has evolved to include owning privately held businesses. This is similar to a PEG in that the owners will not be active day to day and will want a full management team. Correspondingly, they will tend to want to buy and hold (versus buy and flip), they may get younger family members involved, and they may involve their family office management firm in the operations or management of the firm. The size deal they will do depends on the size of the family's investment pool.

Fundless sponsors are similar to PEGs or search fund buyers, although they don't have the money in place yet. They line up possible investors, and when they find a potential deal they go to their investors to gauge interest. There's not too much downside to you with this, other than they may ask for a longer due diligence and no-shop time period while they solidify their funding.

This brings us to one final point on financial buyers. As a seller, you need to perform due diligence on the buyer just like the buyer does on your company. Learn about the buyer's ownership style early in the relationship-building stage: the two extremes are visionary and CMB (cover my butt). Many things in life require a balance; some business owners are too visionary, always going for the home run while ignoring the day to day and its corresponding cash flow, and some focus too much on the minutia while the company stagnates.

Real-Life Story

I knew one such "unbalanced" business owner. For five years his company suffered declining sales and disappearing cash flow while he spent no time on generating new customers or markets. Instead he "bragged" that, while it had taken him two hours, he'd reconciled a twenty-nine-cent difference between the accounts receivable ledger and the customer records.

Here is a quick note on foreign buyers. There is a US law that grants permanent residency to approved foreigners who invest a certain amount of money in businesses that create a minimum number of jobs. As a seller, this is not a buyer market you can target, but these people are out there. They will have many of the same criteria as the financial buyers above and perhaps some of the criteria that strategic buyers have, which are described in the next section.

Strategic buyers

A seller often sees strategic buyers, often corporations, as the panacea. They will come swooping in with piles of cash and give it to you in a very rich deal. Sometimes this happens, but they have their own very specific criteria and yes, you may get that great deal if your business has what the buyer wants (but it doesn't always work that way).

These are often the larger company in the same industry or vertical. They are looking for the following criteria in a potential business purchase:

- Growth potential, or, as one buyer told me, "If we pay seven times EBITDA and grow the business like we want to, it's a great deal. If we pay four times EBITDA and it doesn't grow, it's a bad deal."

- A good management structure in place. Strategic buyers and private equity groups (PEGs) usually don't want to come in and run the company on a day-to-day basis. They want a proven team in place. This carries down to the nonmanagement employees also. They are really buying people (as are all buyers, but it's more pronounced here).

- Correspondingly, the business can't be highly dependent on the seller, whether the seller is staying on as an employee or exiting after transition. A situation like this is often referred to as "personal goodwill" and does not provide the value, or price, associated with "company goodwill." (In simple terms, goodwill is the difference between the value of the assets of the company and the company's value based on other valuation methods (the value created by profit). It should be obvious that a key to avoiding dependencies like this is to have good systems in place and to be using them correctly.

- While profits are important, gross margin may be more important. These buyers can control and reduce the overhead. They don't want customers accustomed to paying so low a price they can't make an acceptable margin.

- Assimilating overhead is often the key component to a deal, even if it's a small or midsized business buying another small business. Combining facilities, reducing administrative staff, or getting increased buying power can all affect the price.

Finally, here is one factor that often gets overlooked but can be the key to postdeal success: company culture. This arises more in larger deals, but it is always a factor. In the February 2010 edition of *Mergers & Acquisitions*, Jonathan Marino, in his article, "Mega Mistakes," writes that the deals that are not successful are the very large deals that "seem to be driven by managerial motives be it empire building or hubris." He quotes Randy Schwimmer, senior managing director and head of capital markets for Churchill Financial, who says, "Companies get into trouble when they don't stick to their knitting." To me, this means they stray off target and ignore, among other things, the culture of their acquisition.

That said, if your company has the size and scope that puts it in a larger firm's acquisition playing field, you have a greater chance of getting a higher price and more cash at closing. Keep in mind, they know the questions to ask and the answers they want to receive and will delve deep during due diligence.

Real-Life Story
A seller told me he didn't know why he should waste his time with an individual financial buyer and the accompanying due diligence when all he had to do was tell firms in his industry he wanted to sell and they would pay him a high price based only on his sales volume. My reply was, "That could happen but probably won't. While they won't have to verify the market demand, the industry, or other things of this nature, they will know all the weak spots your business could have and will pick apart those areas much more deeply than an outside buyer. They know where the secrets can be hidden and how to expose them." He ended up selling to the financial buyer.

Have a process to manage your preparation

Let's conclude this chapter on planning with a short overview of a process to use when preparing your business for sale. There will be more on each of these subjects in later chapters, so this is simply a preview.

Selling a business is tough. Even profitable, well-run companies must overcome obstacles on the way to a win-win deal. Examples of obstacles include the following (you will recognize some of these from above):

- Profits drive the price. If you don't have high profits, you better have something else to create value. This could be proprietary products, proprietary technology, or an unexploited niche.

- While buyers want a well-run, profitable company, they also want scalability. If you present your company as running at maximum efficiency and dominating a market, you will scare away those buyers who fear any change will cause profits to decrease (and they've paid based on the high profits) or that there will be a high cost to growth.

- A buyer's skills and interests must match the attributes needed to run the business. The business cannot be extremely dependent on any one thing (no management structure, a dominant customer, a restrictive lease, etc.).

- The more dependent the business is on the owner, the less attractive it is to buyers.

Ask yourself, if you were on the other side of the table, buying a business, which of the following would you be more comfortable with?

"The business is really a lot better than it looks on paper. There's a lot of potential—we just don't work very hard. The cash flow is higher than you might think, if you don't count my kids' salary, my spouse's car, my insurance, our travel, and other things we deduct. Someone with any marketing skills will do much better than I do."

"We started planning for an exit three years ago. I didn't have immediate plans to sell but wanted to be ready. I have an excellent management team, we've managed our costs and margins efficiently, and our profits (on our tax return) are higher than the industry average. We've been growing steadily, although the growth rate was down a little during the recession, and the systems are in place for a new owner to continue that growth."

ACTION plan to sell a business

To maximize price and streamline the selling process, a business seller should follow an ACTION plan. Follow this plan and you will set yourself apart from other sellers. ACTION stands for the following:

- **Arrange** all the company's affairs

- **Coach** and counsel the company: its people and how those people best use the firm's processes, and systems

- **Transmit** and teach all the good "things" about your firm (and those "things" are:)

- **Intricacies** that make your company special

- **Operations** and management systems in place for a smooth transition

- **Numbers**, all the financials in understandable form, straightforward with no "tricks"

This chapter is about arranging the company's affairs as you prepare it for sale. What's involved in this, the most important component of an ACTION plan? Pay close attention to these areas of the company:

- Nonfinancial factors

- Marketing plan and efforts

- Management structure

- Processes and systems

- Financial systems and reporting

- Risk factors, both internal and external

The nonfinancial factors include, but are not limited to, employees, customers, suppliers, the competition, and your lease. People are a business's top asset, especially in the early twenty-first century. Whether the unemployment rate is high or low, when you have good employees you have a valuable asset, and you have to do what it takes to keep them. You want stable and loyal employees. They are valuable and a necessity.

Management structure is a key to getting a high price and preparing a smooth transition. Whether your buyer is an individual (a financial buyer) or a company (a strategic buyer) no one wants to see a one-person show. If you can take a vacation for one, two, or even three months and upon your return the company is stronger than when you left, you have quality management.

Don't limit your preparation to only the business. You must have your personal life, goals, and objectives in order also. It is very important to work with your attorney, financial planner, and family members to make sure your business goals are in line with your personal goals and financial needs.

Real-Life Story

An owner had plans to sell his business, scale back his life, and do some missionary work with his church. He had accepted an offer from a buyer and calculated how much he would need to live on. It was then that he realized just how lucrative his business was. He had only been considering his salary and medical benefits but never stopped to think about all the perks he and his family enjoyed. He realized he couldn't afford to sell it (even at a fair price) because his lifestyle was higher than he had assumed it was.

Let's expand on the ACTION plan. Having management, processes, and systems is not enough. **Arranging** means you must massage and structure them so they happen automatically.

Coaching is, to use an old cliché, getting the left hand to know what the right hand is doing. The marketing plan and production must relate. It doesn't do any good to generate scores of new customers every month if you can't provide them the best in product or service. Production can't be so far ahead of marketing that inventory regularly piles up and puts the cash flow into disarray. A smoothly running business takes teamwork between people and between systems.

Transmitting means presenting. A buyer must see the company for what it is. Present a good company accurately and buyers will want it more, not less. Show the potential, but have supporting research. Potential is the word most overused by business sellers. Every seller believes his company is worth more because of what it can, or may, do in the future.

The basics of presenting your company to a buyer include covering the obvious things like sales, profits, and product or service. Go into detail, without giving away any trade secrets. Astute buyers will notice this. Remember, when buyers have to dig for information, they always wonder why the information was so hard to get and what else could be hiding.

What exactly should you transmit to a buyer? Start by determining your logical buyer. Is it an individual or small business that needs profit based on the way you're doing business now? Or is it a large corporation that will consolidate, absorb overhead, and seek rocketship growth?

The **intricacies** that make your company special (and profitable) along with the operations are truly the key Let's look at some specifics (this is not an exhaustive list):

- **Pricing**—What if you determined that the price for your product really didn't matter (within limits). People buy it if they want it. Therefore, you can price your product at the upper end of the market range, provide exceptional service (that you couldn't provide at a lower price point), and limit the number of customers. How do you price your services?

- **Planning and structure**—A business buyer, now an owner, updated me on his first year in his business. He explained how he'd improved margins, expanded his sales channels, streamlined the inventory system, and tightened up the financial controls. He concluded by saying, "Just like in the business plan I wrote prior to the purchase."

- **Service**—As I mentioned above, provide exceptional service. You want your clients saying, "I can't believe the service they provide. They take care of every little detail, and then some." This instills loyalty. Think of the little extras that will keep regulars coming back.

- **Marketing**—Use effective market research to determine how to meet your buyers. For example, know which trade shows to participate in and what to do at the shows. Do you regularly research the market and competitors and survey your customers?

- **Technology**—How about a technology that shaves weeks off production time and saves thousands of employee hours and many thousands of dollars? Isn't that a great value point the company has to offer customers? What technology are you using that increases productivity and job security, reduces theft, helps your customers, and ultimately increases profits?

- **Operational structure**—Do you have an organizational chart? Is there proper delegation? Do your employees accept delegation? Do they operate as a team? Again, don't let the company be dependent on the owner. A buyer wants a smooth transition with structure in place. Can you meet that goal?

Your **numbers** are a huge factor in the purchase decision, and your financial statements should be straightforward and accurate. I've seen too many businesses that sold for less than they could have because their accounting system was sloppy and financial statements were not perceived as accurate. One client lost his two top acquisition prospects because he refused to get his financial statements in order, after a year of prodding, pleading, and pressure. He finally sold for a low down payment and the balance on an earn-out.

I tell my audience, "Ignore your CPA!" Just kidding! Your CPA advises you on how to minimize taxes, but you want to pay taxes because you have profits. Show a high owner's salary. Minimize the blending of business and personal expenses. This makes it easy for a buyer to justify the cash flow and your price—and banks love it!

Savvy business buyers look for situations where the seller is forced to sell. Selling a business is not like selling a house. You can't fix, paint, landscape, and have it ready in a couple months. It may take two to three years to make it presentable. Especially if you've been "playing games" with your reported income.

Why plan and prepare? Statistics tell us that nationally, only 10 to 25 percent of businesses whose owners want to sell are ready to sell for maximum price. With an estimated half of all small businesses expected to sell in the next decade, it pays to be ready so you aren't caught in a buyers' market.

Having an ACTION plan assures you won't rush the process, creating buyer suspicion and a lower price. Companies that sell, and especially those that sell at or near their asking price, are those that pay attention to the details mentioned here. As with anything, doing it right the first time is a lot easier, more efficient, and more profitable.

Chapter Two

Double your business; triple your price

Want to read over one million books on how to grow your business? Of course not, and yet there are over one million resources on Amazon.com when you search three words: marketing, sales, and finance.

Want to grow your business? Of course you do. Want to dramatically increase the value of your business? There is no end to the help available if you want to do the same old, same old, just like almost all other businesses. Increase your sales, adjust your pricing, offer more value, pay attention to your people, have a business plan, accelerate your marketing, pay attention to your finances, and so on.

Don't get me wrong, these are important subjects, and we'll briefly discuss how they fit into an exit plan in subsequent chapters. But they are what everybody is preaching and doing (or at least trying to do).

There are numerous strategies to grow a business. Let's cover some of them, and then we'll discuss how you can break away from the pack. Common strategies include the following:

- Add new products or services (or start making more products).

- Expand geographically by sending salespeople on the road more often.
- Open an office in another city.
- Hire more salespeople and hope they can sell.
- Steal customers by (maybe) getting into price wars with the competition.
- Buy more equipment (a sunk cost) so you produce more widgets cheaper.

Real-Life Story

Many years ago I came across a business that was in a world of hurt. Your first thought may be, "Why buy a business that is hurting?" Well, it's because of why it was hurting. The seller expanded into a new geographic area by opening a new office and hiring people. He was not capable of managing those people from a distance, and the new office was failing. Then his ego got involved. He insisted he could "sell" his way out of the problem and also bought an office building in that market at a market peak.

The buyer bought the original location, not the remote location, with the entire down payment going to the state for back taxes, the key vendor, and the telephone company. One of the key motivators was the State of Washington's Department of Revenue. They were ready to close down the business and sell off the assets for back taxes. They insisted on a letter of intent and closing by certain dates to postpone this. These actions were added motivation for the seller.

Grow then sell–why growth by acquisition works

Why not double your sales in months, not years? Don't slug it out in the trenches; soar above the fray. Merger and Acquisition (M&A) people like buzzwords like rollups and consolidations. To us this means buy another business!

Let's look at twelve reasons why growth by acquisition makes sense and cover the business-buying process, including search, analysis, financing, and due diligence. All the while understanding that the objective of this is to eventually have you on the other side of the transaction with not only knowledge of what the buyer is looking for but the emotions she is experiencing.

Twelve reasons you should consider growing by acquisition:

1. Acquire great talent
2. Diversify your product offerings
3. Vendor relationship strategies
4. Location, location, location
5. Make a competitor go away
6. Same overhead, higher volume
7. Assets are cheaper as a package
8. Synergy
9. Diamonds in the rough
10. Customers

11. Yes, we can!

12. The bigger you are…the better

Acquire great talent

Good employees are hard to find and often are not in the job market. While all buyers want capable employees, most strategic buyers (that may be you) like to see a solid management team in place.

Great employees with industry knowledge and experience are in the job market even less. When you are looking for great salespeople, I believe this is amplified. They won't change if they've got a good thing going.

If you acquire their company and create an atmosphere of growth, those employees will want to stay. While I can't comment on the culture in all companies, I do know that many small family-owned businesses have owners who are coasting. They are doing very well, they aren't working too hard, and they don't want to disrupt the nice moneymaking system they have. The employees may be younger and have more energy and ideas on how to grow and challenge themselves and the firm. To the owner, this could mean a bigger payday, with the corresponding risk of slightly lower profits if the ideas don't work, or a temporary profit reduction as there's an investment in the new idea.

> ***Real-Life Story***
>
> ***I once had two clients (coincidentally, both in LA and both distributors) who hired me to find companies in their specific industries. The prime motivator for both was to acquire great salespeople. They needed people with industry knowledge and experience, and they were having trouble finding people willing to change jobs. Buying another company with a good sales staff made more sense than trying to steal employees.***

Diversify your product offerings

Almost every salesperson has left a client's business thinking, "If only we had the X and Y product line, I could sell it to him, save him money, and make more myself." Of course it's tough to get those product lines, especially if you're starting from zero with the supplier.

So why not buy a firm with those product lines and diversify what your people can sell? It doesn't have to be a huge company; it can be a small company that will have full support of its vendor because you can plug the products into your customer base for almost instantaneous growth (of the new product lines).

The products don't have to be similar. I remember one owner who sold packaging materials (boxes). He believed he could acquire a company that sold any kind of supplies to warehouses. What else do warehouses use? Paper, tape, janitorial supplies, racks, material handling equipment, and more. Don't limit yourself. Think creatively.

Vendor relationship strategies

Diversifying vendors means accessing vendors you can't get on your own. Many have territories and protect their distributors and retailers. Acquiring one of their customers gets you in the door. Once in the door, you can make the most of the opportunity.

All of this assumes you're buying a company with different products than yours. This also works for buying a competitor (or similar business in another market) with the same product line. For retailers, this means buying a store that carries the same lines that you carry. The end result in either case is that you will do higher volumes with your suppliers and qualify for greater (volume) discounts.

Location, location, location

This is the old mantra for retail and it applies to other industries also. There may be a location you want and can't get. It could be a retail location and it could be, for manufacturers and distributors, a building near a distribution center, on a rail line, or close to suppliers. While this may not be common, when combined with some of the other reasons for making an acquisition, it may be your tipping point. More apropos for most companies is to expand geographically by buying a similar business (competitor) in another market.

> ***Real-Life Story***
> ***One of my clients purchased a California business similar to his Seattle company. It gives him added volume and the opportunity for faster growth, and he was able to hire an industry friend to be the chief California salesperson. The acquired firm had no sales team, as the owners, in their seventies, weren't active; they were "coasting."***

Make a competitor go away

Some businesses have more than general industry competition; they have a specific competitor that stands in their way. It may be a fierce rival (along the lines of bitter sports rivals like the Packers and Bears or Yankees and Red Sox) or it may just be that there isn't a big enough market for either firm to break away from the other.

Acquire your competitor (or merge if you're friendly). This may make fast growth easier, cheaper, and more achievable. It may allow for faster moves into other markets or segments using traditional growth strategies. This strategy ties in very well with the previous strategy of expanding geographically by acquisition.

Same overhead, higher volume

Look at all the strategies above and below; 90 percent or more of the time you will add volume without adding the corresponding overhead. This is often one of the prime motivators for making an acquisition. If you have forty employees and two staff accountants, and the other firm has twenty-five employees and two staff accountants, there is a good chance you'll only need three staff accountants after the acquisition. Boom! One salary, tax, and benefit package goes to the bottom line. The same can happen with rent, other staff, phone, Internet, advertising, and more.

Real-Life Story

A client bought one of his suppliers. It was a small business with a lot of inefficiencies. He was able to move the business into his space, replace at least one production worker (my client had capacity), and coordinate marketing efforts with no increase in his marketing costs. In addition, just think of all the other overhead he could eliminate, including telephone lines, accounting services, and utilities. He took a sleepy little company and turned almost all of its gross profit into pure net profit.

Assets are cheaper as a package

Tangible assets are a sunk cost. Once you have them, whether it's vehicles, machines, forklifts, or space, you have the cost or payments. You need to make them efficient. All businesses struggle with this for tangible and human assets.

At some point you have to buy a new machine (or hire a new person) because you're over capacity on current equipment, people are working too much overtime, or some other reason. However, once you buy that piece of equipment your capacity increases and your utilization drops. You have to generate more sales to get the equipment running at a profitable rate.

Wouldn't it be nice if the equipment, just like people, came with sales orders? Of course it would, and that's why buying another company can be a good way to get needed equipment with corresponding customers. As the header for this section states, these assets can be cheaper as a package (versus buying new or used assets that don't come with customers).

Synergy

In an oversimplified example, you sell paper and the company down the street sells envelopes. You sell to the same customer base. Wouldn't it make sense for one salesperson, not two, to call on each customer and sell paper and envelopes? The same holds true for delivery people, warehouse people, and accounting (one monthly invoice, not two).

These situations don't come up every day. Savvy owners are always on the lookout for them though. It doesn't have to be as blatant an example as paper and envelopes. My story above about a packaging company seeking a firm that sells completely different products (like janitorial supplies) to the same customers can work just as well.

Diamonds in the rough

This may mean buy a loser, it may mean buy a struggling business (personal income to the owner but no real profit), or it could be buying a business where you can see things that can be done to make it more than it is now.

Often the loser business has no options other than to struggle along, close the doors, or sell to another business. Rarely will individuals or other financial buyers (those needing an income from the business) buy a loser. That means their options are very limited as only a small percentage of companies ever consider growth by acquisition, which makes it an even stronger strategy for those who do.

This can be a good find and at a low cost. Perhaps even on an earn-out basis (payments to the seller based on sales or profits or the increase of sales and profits, and the payments are not guaranteed). And these can still be win-win deals. You get volume, people, and more, and the seller gets more money for the company that he wouldn't otherwise have gotten.

Real-Life Story

Technology can often produce large profit growth, even for nontech businesses. A service business with burned-out owners (actually they were well beyond burned out, they were fried) had a website that acted like a brochure. To order services the customers had to call in, and we all know how that works—repeated phone tag.

Even if an order is left on voice mail, it has to be confirmed. In any event, it takes an employee to process the order and the customer has to take time to make the calls, return calls, and talk about the order. The buyer noticed this during analysis and within months had an online ordering system. It saved the customers' time and hassle, and it increased his staff's productivity a lot. It's not rocket science; it's observing and looking at things through the customers' eyes.

Now here are the top three reasons to grow by acquisition.

Customers

"This would be a great business if it wasn't for those darn customers" was a semiserious comment someone made to me years ago. Of course it's the annoying (bad) customers he was referring to. It's good customers we all want more of—customers who are loyal, steady, in good financial shape, growing, pay their bills on time, appreciate the value you offer, and consider you part of their team.

I mentioned above that acquiring a new product or service line that you can sell to your customers is a good reason for an acquisition. The same holds true for selling your current offerings to a new group of customers. Often this can be done without any increase in your sales force.

An ideal situation is where there are some overlapping products, so there is some continuity and synergy to be achieved. The figure below shows this. Your salespeople now have an easy transition to discussing, and selling, their products, and their salespeople have an easy transition to discussing, and selling, your products.

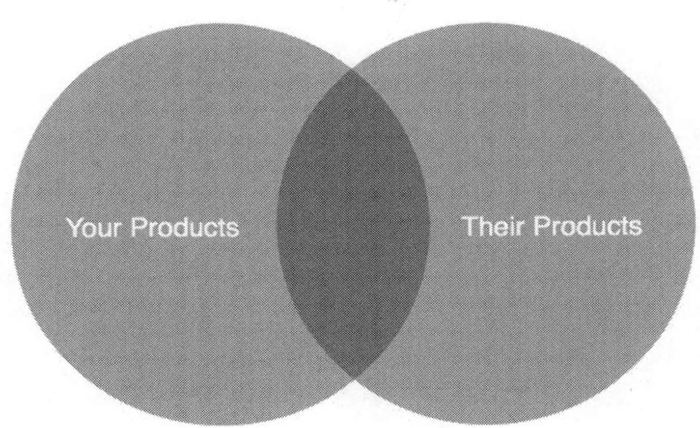

In simple terms, if your primary motivation is acquiring a customer base, you are acquiring market share. You may have many other reasons (geographic expansion, talent acquisition, etc.), but the bottom line is you are buying customers, and that means top-line growth.

Yes, we can!

This is not about ego; it is about building an exit strategy and getting a higher selling price. Buying another company, assimilating it into your operation, and showing that the combined profits are greater than the two individual companies' profits demonstrates to potential buyers that this can be done. It proves you have the team that can integrate one operation into another.

This integration could be their assimilating your firm into theirs or it could be a signal that growing your business (or now a division of theirs) is possible by further acquisitions. A management team that can successfully integrate other firms without major disruption and with immediate efficiencies is a valued team. Too many big mergers and acquisitions fail. Up to 95 percent of public mergers do not live up to expectations. A savvy buyer will appreciate this talent and experience.

Real-Life Story

Keith bought a small business. The company manufactured a handful of proprietary products; the business was overly dependent on the seller, his products, and manufacturing skills; and it was marginally profitable, meaning there were small profits after paying the owner a fair market salary for his work. Bottom line, it was a great deal for both sides.

This was Keith's second acquisition; his first was described in chapter one. Three years prior he'd bought a decades-old manufacturing and distribution company.

The small manufacturing business that was his second acquisition was one of the suppliers for the distribution side of his company. He knew the product, its potential, its weaknesses, and how to sell more of it than the seller was selling. This acquisition was also part of his overall exit strategy as it showed he could purchase a company, absorb it into his operation (profitably), and increase his rate of return on assets and sales.

For the seller, Keith was a lifesaver. Who else was going to buy a company so dependent on the owner's product development skills and product knowledge? Surely not an individual wanting to own her own business. Not another company without any insight into the product and its markets. And, the seller got a consulting job with Keith to engineer the products he invented and the products Keith's company already made.

Why larger firms sell for more than smaller ones (all other things being equal)

The bigger your business is, the more it will sell for, all other things being equal. A $50 million (revenue) company with 10 percent EBITDA will sell for a higher multiple than a $25 million company with 10 percent EBITDA, which will sell for a higher multiple than a $15 million company, and so on.

There are generally accepted ranges for multiples of EBITDA based on the range of companies' revenue. However, too many owners see in the *Wall Street Journal* that a $250 million company in their industry sold for ten times EBITDA and assume their small business will also sell for ten times. That won't happen; there's more risk in smaller businesses than larger, so the desired return on investment is higher.

> ***Real-Life Example***
> ***Companies with sales of $5 to 50 million tend to sell for four to seven times EBITDA, with those on the higher end of EBITDA selling for a higher multiple. Grow your $5 million company to $15 million and your multiple may increase by one times EBITDA (from four to five, for example). Assuming 10 percent profit (and a four multiple) you can see the price go from $2 million to $7.5 million (10 percent profit at five times).***

The fastest and safest way to grow from $5 to 15 million is by acquisition. Buy another firm in your industry—a supplier, customer, or unrelated company that provides diversification—to have an immediate revenue increase and a larger platform from which to grow organically. See more profit and a higher multiple when you exit.

"It's not bragging if you can do it." (Dizzy Dean, 1934)

A lot of business owners talk about their company's potential or the growth that will occur if the buyer just "does some marketing." Of course, most of this is just talk. Business buyers of all types and sizes are a skeptical lot. When they hear too much about potential they think the seller has tried every conceivable way to grow and can't.

So prove you can do it. Go out and buy another company. Show that you can integrate the people, processes, financial systems, customer service, and everything else into your operation. Private equity groups and large corporations make multiple acquisitions. If you can buy another firm and successfully assimilate it, you become more attractive to these buyers. They will assume you can do it again and that your management team is capable. Strategic buyers and equity group buyers highly value management teams—it can even increase the multiple (compared to having the same size company that has not made acquisitions).

Create a breath of fresh air

The sales manager at a recently acquired firm thanked me for getting the deal done and said that the new buyer was a breath of fresh air. The new owner, unlike the seller, listened to the employees' ideas, let them act on them, and was willing to take risks. Too often employees get in a rut. They like the company and their jobs, but it gets to be routine. When the boss ignores them, they lose enthusiasm and leave.

You can inject a breath of fresh air by buying another business. Enthusiasm is hard to teach and it's contagious. The excitement of an acquisition can fire up your team and the team of the acquired business with a new and rewarding challenge. Often their company is being sold because the owner is retiring or burned out. In either event, that owner has probably been coasting while the employees are constantly having new ideas. Put two fired-up teams together and let them use their abilities and you have 2+2=22.

		Skill	
		+	-
Energy	+	2+2=22	2+2=4
	-	2+2=4	2+2=0

Ready, set, go–the business buying process

So now that you've decided this is a strategy worth exploring, what do you do next? The goal is to find a motivated seller with synergies. Sellers who can't articulate why they are selling or what they will do after they sell have a greater chance of backing out or getting seller remorse (backing out of a deal is the ultimate seller remorse).

This is why you need a good search system—so you will find more than one candidate. If one deal falls through, it's not back to square one, it's move on to the next. (Don't forget all of this when you are selling. At that point you will need to be truly motivated, want a choice of buyers, and have reasonable expectations.)

Following is a nine-step acquisition sequence. Secure an experienced guide and pay attention to the details and it will lead to a good acquisition. These are the nine steps:

1. Preparation

2. Search and screening

3. Finance

4. Analyze

5. Value and pricing

6. Deal making

7. Negotiation

8. Due diligence

9. Transition planning

Of course there's a tenth step, and that is closing. Since that's the goal, we won't count it as an action step.

Real-Life Story

Three is a good number of candidates to have in the queue. I remember when one of my clients had his first deal collapse. He moved on to the second company, and as we got close to making a deal, the seller realized that his compensation was much more than just his salary and he couldn't afford to sell. His lifestyle had gotten ahead of him. When this happened I phoned my client and suggested he call candidate three, a company on his back burner as he investigated others. He replied, "I already have a meeting with them on Friday." He had that meeting and closed on the deal two months later.

Preparation

Chapter one gave some statistics on why exit planning makes sense. Don't show this book (and especially chapter one) to any companies on your target list! You want the owner who urgently wants to sell and hasn't taken the time to do what you are doing.

To capitalize on this, you need to prepare more than ever. Preparation means defining as many criteria as you can upfront and being as wide as you possibly can be with those criteria. Most privately owned businesses, 94 percent, have sales of under $10 million. That means there are smaller deals available that you may be able to get for a good price and use as a base for your traditional growth strategies. This can be a lot more effective than stretching to buy the largest business you can afford, and it carries less risk of transition shock.

Define the basics of a desired acquisition, like geographic area, size range, acceptable profit range, and industry. Does it do exactly what you do? Is it a customer, a vendor, unrelated to your business? Then move into the softer criteria:

- What strengths do you want the management team and employees to have?
- What kind of customers should the target firm have?
- Will the seller be expected to stay on or will she leave ASAP?

The more you prepare before searching, the better results you will have.

Search and screening

Career coaches and outplacement agencies teach their job-seeking executives great skills, including interview techniques and negotiating. However, as important as those skills are, they are useless if the executive doesn't interview with companies or get job offers. The same is true for the rest of the acquisition sequence. Deal structure and expertise is useless if you don't find a company. A solid, proven search system is the key.

The purpose of this book is to show you how to do what homeowners do when selling their house. Spiff it up, make it look good on the surface and underneath the surface so it passes inspection (known as due diligence in buy-sell transactions). You know that's not easy, and so the chances are good your acquisition candidate will not have done the work you are doing (or going to do). If you find a prepared business, great; if not, perhaps that means there is all the more opportunity.

In simple terms, finding a company to acquire that meets your criteria means you (pick your favorite cliché) beat the bushes, pound the streets, or turn over every rock to see if there is a motivated seller to be found. Often the seller is scared, scared to death in some cases, that somebody (anybody) will find out the business may be for sale. And that fear is legitimate. Employees get scared if they perceive big change, competitors will use it against them, and vendors may put them on COD.

Real-Life Story

James was selling his small business to a larger competitor. Against my advice he told his two key employees he was going to be selling (before he had a deal). Within thirty days both gave their notice, although they ended up staying.

An owner told me that he shared with a supplier that he was "thinking" of selling. The vendor put him on COD. When I shared that when speaking to a group of accountants, a lady in the back squirmed in her seat with her hand in the air. (I thought I'd missed the time for the break.) She wanted to tell me that her firm sold through distributors, and if they knew one was selling, their policy was also to put it on COD.

The above points out that finding a business is hard work. It takes focus. It's not something you (or your staff or your acquisition advisor) do sporadically or haphazardly. Finding a company is like a sales effort. You have to work your (prospecting) system consistently and constantly. This is tough while running a business. Assign tasks just like you would any growth effort, monitor it, and track activities and results.

So, where are they? Where are all these great acquisition candidates? They are everywhere, which is why it is so tough to find them. There is no central listing like the Multiple Listing Service for real estate. Even if there were, it wouldn't help you too much because only one in five small to medium-sized businesses are sold by a broker (this statistic is from the business brokers trade groups). That means you have to find the other 80 percent. That's why I say it's a sales effort. You and your employees are all acting like salespeople, except instead of prospecting for new customers, you are prospecting for business sellers.

The first and easiest place to start is with the business brokers and M&A department of investment banking firms (the ones appropriate for your size deal). Call every intermediary you can find in every city in which you are willing to buy a company. Determine which ones work with the type and size of firm you are targeting. The key is to stay in touch. Call them once a month to let them know you're serious.

If you want to buy a company in your industry or a related industry, use your industry connections. Trade groups, professional groups, and professionals (accountants, consultants, attorneys, and others) can all be good sources. Start by contacting the national, regional, and local offices of any trade groups you belong to. If you aren't a member, join. If you aren't an active member, get active. Become known, especially to the executive director and key staff. When they see you do good work for the association, they will feel much better about helping you and referring companies to you.

You should also tell everybody you know that you are seeking to grow by acquisition. Don't be bashful; many deals are found because of the "people" factor. You never know who knows somebody who knows somebody who knows an owner wishing to retire or sell for other reasons. One client found the business he bought by sending an e-mail to an alumni group. One of his fellow alumni forwarded it to others and one of those recipients introduced him to an owner who not only wanted to sell but also sold to him.

Finally, realize that finding a business to buy is a contact sport. The more contacts you make, the better your chances of finding a company. Many years ago an investment banker told me that the common impression of his profession was that it was always glamorous and exciting. He went on to say he spent most of his time at his desk "dialing for dollars." In other words, working his contacts and others who might be able to help him. Get a list of target companies and contact them. Whether you write or call, make contacts.

Making contacts brings up an interesting point. Who makes all these contacts? You can. Or your management team can. But do you or your staff have the time? What about confidentiality? For example, if one of your competitors called you and asked if you were interested in merging or selling, what would you say? If you're like most owners you would immediately say, "Not interested" because it could be a fishing expedition and that competitor could tell customers your business is for sale. What if you didn't know who was calling—would you be any more relaxed about saying you'll discuss selling your business? This can be a tough subject, can't it?

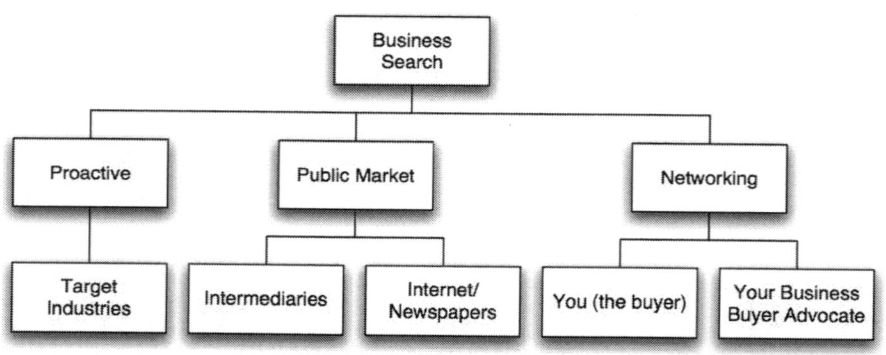

That's where an intermediary comes into play. Somebody who does this every day can better protect a seller's confidentiality. Since the business is based on keeping secrets, using an intermediary opens up doors to places you can't get into. I recommend you find an intermediary who does predominantly buy-side representation and works in the deal size range you are targeting. Industry knowledge often takes a backseat to transaction knowledge. In addition, someone too well known in an industry may know too much or too many people. As Benjamin Franklin said, "Three people can keep a secret if two of them are dead." Getting an industry outsider on your team may be the smartest thing you do.

To summarize, the following are some tips for searching for a business:

- Approach it the same way you approach any sales or marketing function.

- There has to be a plan and you (and your team) have to follow the plan and pay attention to the details.

- Your goal is to get in front of sellers in situations where you are the only buyer talking to them.

- It takes time, hard work, and smart work.

- You'll kick a lot of tires, but it'll be well worth it when you find the right match.

Screening

The most important part of the screening process is screening the individual (or individuals) selling the business. While at some point you will do a credit check and related background research, the first step is to find out if you are compatible with the seller.

Not only will you be working with the seller for months (or years) during transition or if she becomes employed by your firm, but also think about it from this perspective: The seller has relationships with customers, vendors, and employees. If she gets along with them and you don't get along with the seller or your styles are completely different, then how are you going to relate to the customers, vendors, and employees? That creates a culture clash, the issue that derails, or at the very least disrupts, large corporate mergers.

This means your first job when you meet a seller is to build some rapport. Find out if your styles and personalities are compatible. Not only can this make or break a deal, it can make or break the postdeal success.

During the search process, we defined acquisition criteria and the basic search criteria of location, size, and type of business. You don't need to do too much more in this area, as the objective is to cast a wide net and filter out those that don't meet your deeper criteria. Some of the criteria at the next level include the following:

- Cash flow or profit—do you need to buy a profitable company? Is it worth looking into companies that are breaking even or losing money if you can absorb them and eliminate their overhead? Have an acceptable range and use it when screening companies. One caveat is not to eliminate companies too early. Unfortunately, many owners don't know their exact profit situation and some, to protect themselves, won't give an accurate number too soon in the discussions.

- What type of ownership structure are you willing to accept? In other words, are you looking for a pure acquisition or would a merger work (especially with you retaining majority interest and control)?

- What type of management team and key employees are you looking for? For example, if your company is great at operations and your weakest area is sales, you may want to buy a firm with a strong sales department. Or maybe you just want added volume or line workers. Know what you want going in.

Don't be afraid to ask yourself and the seller thought-provoking questions like, "What do you do on a daily basis?" If you are buying a firm that is different from your firm (even if it's a supplier or customer), ask the owner about barriers to entry in his niche or how he attracts customers (relationship or marketing—there's a big difference). Your objective is to eliminate candidates, for legitimate reasons, as soon as possible.

And while you're planning, think about the answers you will give to questions you get from the seller. The right answer could solidify your deal. The wrong answer could kill it, and who knows how long it will take to find another qualified company. You don't want to divulge too much about you and your business too soon. Confidentiality is a two-way street.

The following sections on the acquisition sequence will be shorter than the sections on search and screening. This is for three reasons:

1. Search is the most important factor; you can't buy a company until you find one.

2. The purpose of this book is to extensively cover how you will escape from your company; it is not meant to be a guide on buying one (a possible preliminary step in your exit strategy).

3. There's a lot of information out there on analyzing companies, and you probably know a lot of what you want in a candidate.

Financing

Financing is always important to getting a deal done. Without knowing your size, structure, or cash position, I offer four basic guidelines:

1. Cash talks, and the more cash a seller gets at closing the lower the price can be.

2. Providing stock, equity in your firm, can have advantages: a lower cash outlay, lower debt (which your bank will like), and it will keep the seller onboard for years, if that's what you want.

3. Bank loans are available for acquisitions, and as of this writing the limit on SBA guaranteed loans is $5 million. SBA guaranteed loans generally carry a longer term, up to ten years, than a conventional loan but have higher fees.

4. Look for the cash flow or assets of the business to help pay for the business. This is creative financing. Every deal is different and often there are ways to get cash out of the business at closing or just after.

Real-Life Story

Robb bought a business where the seller loved assets. He loved seeing racks full of inventory. In his first year, Robb sold off $200,000 of inventory that he did not replace. Instead he managed inventory better. That inventory turned into cash on his balance sheet and in his bank account.

Numerous deals include cash and accounts receivable. This allows the buyer to finance some of the working capital over an extended period of time (or pull some of the cash out).

Analyze

Analysis is the next step, although at this point all the remaining "steps" in the process become intermingled, as we'll see. Unfortunately, this step is where many deals unnecessarily lose momentum. Too often the buyer wants too much information too soon and it spooks the seller. Remember, you may have just met the seller—it's probably premature to ask her to expose all of her business secrets to you.

That's why I advise a stepped approach. It starts with taking a look at the financial statements and working with the seller to "recast" or adjust them so you can see the true profit picture of the business. By this I mean, you want to know what the bottom line would be if the business tried to show as much profit as possible instead of paying as little tax as possible. This means looking for those "lifestyle" expenses that many business owners run through their company. It also means adjusting the depreciation and anticipated capital expenditure categories and looking for expenses that will disappear or will have to be added when you are the owner.

At the same time, ask some big-picture questions about all the nonfinancial aspects of the business. For example (and there are all-encompassing questions for all categories in the appendices), the following are questions we ask about the technology side of the business:

- Is your technology up to date?
- Are any subscriptions not current?
- Are there any virus or security issues?
- Does any hardware or software need upgrading (is the hardware less than three years old)? If yes, please explain the situation and the estimated cost.

A yes answer lets you probe deeper. A no answer lets you feel comfortable until it comes time to delve in deeper. As we ask these big-picture questions, we let the seller know we will accept her answers, base a deal on those answers, and then prove what she told us during due diligence. We'd prefer to hear any "bad news" now instead of being surprised in due diligence, which is a time for confirmation, not discovery.

Value versus price

Valuation is covered in chapter eight, so let me just comment on value versus price. Value is based on formulas and methodologies. Value takes into account both the financial and the nonfinancial factors. Price is the perceived value agreed upon by the buyer and the seller. The price can be, and often is, different from the value because value is theoretical and price is real-world.

How the price is paid, as mentioned above, affects price (not value). Motivation and need affect price (not value). A seller who needs a certain amount of cash at closing may sell for a lower overall price. A buyer with less cash or who really needs to fill a gap in his business (via this acquisition) may pay more. Always seek counsel from a transaction tax expert on this subject.

Deal-making and negotiation

There are three components to all deals: price, terms, and conditions. Price and terms are pretty self-explanatory. Conditions vary from deal to deal. Conditions could include employment contracts with key employees, environmental reports, due diligence issues specific to the company, lease extensions, or many other things.

As you get ready to formulate a deal structure that will lead to an offer, here are three things to do:

1. Consult someone in the valuation field and perhaps get a limited opinion of value.

2. Start talking to bankers. Even if you don't plan to use a bank to help finance the deal, I recommend you talk to some. They look at companies and deals differently than entrepreneurs do.

3. Work with your acquisition advisor or team and your management team to formulate a value range and decide how much cash you plan to invest.

Some banks love acquisition loans and some don't quite understand them. Your bank may be great to work with, but if it doesn't have a history and culture of liking acquisition loans, you might not get very far. Do some research and find out which banks (and bankers) understand and like these loans. Some banks only care about assets, some only care about cash flow, and many are in the middle, meaning they want some of both. Play the field, as you never know what will happen and the banks approach to acquisition loans is often a key component to getting a loan and a deal.

Real-Life Story

The owner of two very successful businesses with a long entrepreneurial track record was purchasing another unrelated business. He worked closely with one large bank while keeping others in the wings. The loan officer, credit manager, and committee liked the deal and it went to HQ for final approval. As I understand it, it passed muster at the first three levels and then the final decision maker at the corporate HQ rejected the loan saying, "I never liked that industry."

This caused a lot of broken hearts (buyer, banker, seller) and it was on to another bank. The community bank that did the deal looked at the buyer's history of being an entrepreneur as much as anything ("character" is the term used) and made the loan.

We are often talking about small, relationship-based deals here. If the negotiations get contentious or the attorneys get involved in negotiating deal points (not legal points), it can be tough to get the deal back on track. That's why it is often beneficial for both sides to have an intermediary on their team. The intermediary can wear the "black hat" and be the bad guy (or gal) and also has the knowledge and experience to mitigate potential problems and disarm minor issues that the inexperienced person might magnify out of proportion. There are often "behind-the-scenes" discussions that keep the deal on track without letting the buyer or seller's emotions take center stage.

Real-Life Story

One of my most memorable experiences in this area took place in a coffee shop. I was representing the seller, and when the meeting was over he turned to me and said, "You earned your

whole fee in this meeting." What did I do? I convinced the seller that good buyers with money, skill, interest in your business, and whom you like don't come along often. I convinced the buyer that good businesses you can afford, that you feel comfortable running, and where you like the seller don't come along often. So, to both parties, I made the point that it could be a long time before either of them met another great match, so they should do everything possible to get the deal done. The deal closed the next month.

One final word on this subject: the deal has to work for you. It also has to work for the seller. Emotions get in the way, so don't get unrealistic buyer fever. As a buyer, hope the seller likes you so much she gives you an asking price that is more than fair (which does happen fairly often).

Due diligence

As with valuation, volumes have been written on due diligence. A master due diligence list with some standard due diligence topics and questions is provided in Appendix A. Appendix B is a list of nonfinancial questions to use when meeting with a seller. Once a deal structure is agreed to, a nonbinding letter of intent (LOI) signed, and the purchase and sale agreement is being drafted, it is time for due diligence. Whether on the buy or sell side of the table, you should expect these questions.

Due diligence is the process of proving what you've been told (the facts on which you based the offer). During the process you may also uncover some risks that may cause you to change or kill the deal, or you may uncover opportunities you didn't know about.

If you're thinking, "Shouldn't I be performing due diligence before I make an offer?" consider it from the seller's perspective. If you were the seller, and you will be someday, would you let a buyer talk to your employees, customers, vendors, or landlord before you had a deal in place? Would you want a buyer "auditing" your books, seeing your business plan, and getting other secrets and strategies from you? This is why you tell the seller, "I will base my offer on this early information and will prove it during due diligence. So please tell me about any things that might concern me now as I don't want to be surprised and have to renegotiate the deal later."

So what exactly is due diligence? In simple terms it is investigating all the details and intricacies of a business to verify the business is what you thought it was (or better than you thought). You will break down the financial statements, prepare a budget, and do a month-by-month cash flow projection. On the nonfinancial side, you will discreetly interview customers (not telling them you are buying the company), talk to the management team and key employees, work with the landlord on your lease, interview vendors, and if there are any contracts, get approval to transfer them to you. In addition you will update or prepare a business plan (for yourself and the bank).

Transition planning

Too often so much emphasis is put on getting the deal closed that the day after closing the buyer shows up and it's "Now what?" Integrating the acquired business with your business the right way will increase the probability that growth and profit expectations and projections will be met. There's a lot more on this in chapter ten so I won't elaborate here.

Buying another business is not for everybody. There are serious risks involved, and that is why the rate of return is much higher than on other investments. However, if you want to grow faster and bigger or to position yourself for an eventual sale, buying another business is probably faster, cheaper, safer, and easier to finance than starting a new division, opening a branch in another city, and increasing your sales and marketing efforts to grow organically.

If you desire any of the goals associated with growth by acquisition, you owe it to yourself to investigate it. Follow a proven plan and pay attention to the details. Put together a team including your attorney, accountant, acquisition advisor, and banker. Make sure all have experience in transactions of the type you are targeting. Keep in mind that preparation and planning make the process go faster and smoother. As the late Lionel Haines (a noted author of many books on the buying and selling of businesses) said, "You must act like a hunter, not a trapper." You have to get out there and actively search for businesses, as you would prospect for new customers. This is not a passive sport.

Once you find a good candidate, don't create your own speed bumps or roadblocks. There are enough already out there! There is risk involved, and if you feel your skills balance the risks of the business you are considering, then delve in and find out what makes that company tick. In other words, why is it profitable or unprofitable? Some of the best deals are when a money-losing company is "saved" by someone in the industry who can make money on the same sales volume (or, as a better manager, do little things that make a big difference).

Chapter Three

Beauty is in the eye of the beholder

Buying another business is great preparation for when you sell, as you'll understand what the buyer is looking for. As a buyer, you'll understand that they are by nature skeptical, and if they are not natural skeptics, they quickly turn into skeptics as they see all the overpriced and unprofitable businesses that dominate the Internet.

Mock due diligence

The next best way to find out what a buyer will see is to put your company through a "mock" due diligence. Everything in this chapter should be viewed with the understanding that a mock due diligence and a buyer's due diligence are very similar. Consider having an outside pair of eyes assist you, as it is human nature to miss things we are closest to.

Your job is to anticipate what a buyer will ask and have the business ready for investigation. We talked about different buyer types and their objectives. As with many things in life, Pareto's Principle holds true here (also known as the eighty-twenty rule). Buyers of all types and sizes will be concerned with the same 80 percent of issues in an acquisition target.

Most potential buyers will not be very interested in doing much legal due diligence because they will not want to buy your stock. There are two types of corporate transactions, a stock sale and an asset sale. The terms relate to how the transaction is taxed, not what the buyer gets.

Transaction structures

Disclaimer: For the sections on deal structure, I am not giving tax or legal advice. I am passing along big-picture information and strategies. Both buyer and seller should have experienced tax and legal advice on all of these matters.

If it's a stock sale, the history of the corporation is very important and the buyer's legal team will be busy. Legal due diligence is negligible if it's an asset sale because the history of the corporation is not very important.

I'm not going to describe legal due diligence because I'm not an attorney. I will describe some basic transaction facts and strategies.

One of the first things a buyer will see or ask about is your business's structure. For corporations there is the option of either a stock or asset sale.

Stock sale

In a stock sale, you are selling the shares of your company just as if you were selling shares in a publicly traded company. If your cost or basis in your firm is $1 million and you sell the shares for $7 million, you have a capital gain of $6 million and (as of this writing) that gain will be taxed at capital gains tax rates.

When you sell shares, you sell everything, including cash, accounts receivable, accounts payable, and other liabilities, in addition to your operating assets like inventory, vehicles, and equipment. (Often the amount of net working capital left in the company is negotiated and part of the contract.) You also are selling future warranty claims, past and future legal claims, and everything else, known and unknown, that goes with the operations of a company (although the buyer's lawyer will protect him on these issues). The latter is one reason buyers don't prefer to buy your stock and why legal bills on a supposedly simpler stock sale are just as high as on an asset sale.

Parts of the "everything" you are selling are the asset values and depreciation schedules on your current balance sheet. If you have $2 million of equipment and it is depreciated down to $200,000, then the buyer gets assets valued at $200,000 and your current depreciation schedule—even if those assets have a fair market value of $1 million.

The following is from my good friend Mike Larson; Mike is a very good and experienced business and transaction attorney in Seattle, WA.

What Is a Stock Sale?

A stock purchase and sale transaction usually involves a shareholder selling her share in the company to another in exchange for a purchase price. This transaction may seem simple, generally only requiring the shareholder to endorse the back of her stock certificate. However, in actuality, the sale of stocks is not a simple transaction at all and requires much thought and consideration on the part of the buyer prior to the actual sale. This is because when buyers purchase stock from a corporation or shares in an LLC, they are essentially purchasing the underlying business and will, therefore, be responsible for all of the liabilities of the company being acquired. Examples include federal and state tax obligations and pending claims and lawsuits from the failure to pay employees and vendors to warranty and other claims. Therefore, in order to protect themselves in such a transaction, they: (1) perform due diligence on the business; (2) properly value the business; (3) request adequate representations and warranties from the seller.

Due Diligence

Due diligence is the investigation and review of a business in connection with a stock sale transaction. Due diligence allows the purchaser and his lawyer to formulate a better understanding of the business and its operations, which will assist him in determining whether to buy the stocks, at what price, and on what terms and conditions. Due diligence is usually done prior to or during the negotiating of definitive documents and includes the investigation and review of the following:

- Financial information (financial statements and tax returns)
- Operational structure of the business:
    - Interviews with management
    - Touring the business facility
    - Review of sales and marketing programs, supplier and customer lists
- Organizational documents
- Debt and equity documentation
- Material contracts
- Employment arrangements, including employee benefit plans
- Real estate and environmental matters
- Intellectual property
- Existing and past lawsuits
- Regulatory compliance

The purchaser or his attorney should consider completing a due diligence checklist prior to entering into a transaction.

Valuation of a Business or Stocks of Business

Another important part of stock sales is valuation of the stocks being purchased. In order to properly value the stocks, one needs to do a proper valuation of the business. Of course, it may not be possible at the beginning of negotiations to know the exact value of the business, therefore, coming up with a range of values should be adequate. An investment banker, an accounting firm, or a company that specializes in valuation services can do a valuation of a business. There are also many different ways to value a business, and some of the more common methods are (1) discounted cash flow approach, (2) historical performance of the company, (3) asset valuation, and (4) industry comparable sales data.

Representations and Warranties

Last but not least, it is always important to the buyer to require the seller make certain representations and/or warranties about the company. There are many reasons why a purchaser should have a seller make representations and warranties, such as to obtain disclosures from the seller about the company, to secure future indemnity rights for any "losses" occurring from a breach of the representations and warranties, **and to possibly have the right to walk away from or rescind the transaction on the basis of breach of warranty, or due to the failure to satisfy a contingency, if the sale transaction differs from what was represented**. Some of the general representations and warranties made by a seller include the following:

- Operation of the business
- Financial and physical condition of the business

- Assets
- Existing lawsuits
- Capitalization of seller
- Affirmation that after due diligence disclosures there is nothing else the buyer has not seen and the seller has not disclosed

A purchaser will try not to have the seller expressly limit her representation to known things. This is because unless the representation or warranty is expressly limited to the seller's knowledge, the purchaser may recover from the seller for misrepresentations *and* incorrect representations as well, even if the seller did not know of the facts and circumstances surrounding the breach. When deciding what kinds of representations or warranties to request from the seller, a buyer might consider whether to set time limits on the representation and/or warranties, whether to set a minimum and maximum amount of liability for the seller, and whether to set a minimum threshold amount of losses incurred by the purchaser before the indemnity clause starts to work. Additionally, the buyer will ask the seller to include in the representations that there is nothing else the purchaser has not seen regarding the business or its operations.

These representations and warranty obligations should be secured by a personal guaranty of the seller, remembering the seller's personal guaranty is only as good as his financial situation. That is another reason a buyer will want to pay part of the purchase price later in a deferred obligation. The deferred obligation, say a promissory note payable over time, provides the buyer some time to discover misrepresentations or nondisclosures of hard-to-discover liabilities and use the deferred payment as a source of compensation from the resulting damages.

In closing, the purchaser will investigate to the best of her abilities and perform due diligence prior to purchasing stock, since the representations and warranties the seller makes are only as good as the person backing them up.

Mike Larson, Pivotal Law Group in Seattle, Washington, www.pivotallawgroup.com, 206-343-2008

Asset sale

Most of the business buyers I meet erroneously assume that an asset sale means they don't get everything in the company, only the tangible assets like inventory and equipment. The term "asset sale" is strictly for tax purposes. The buyer can buy all assets, tangible and intangible, and can even purchase liabilities. It's similar to going to the grocery store and filling your cart with what you want.

Buyers will always want your operational assets and the intangibles like telephone numbers, website URLs, and e-mail addresses. During negotiations you will determine which nonoperational assets the buyer will get; these could include cash, accounts receivable, prepaid expenses, and perhaps even some corresponding liabilities.

Why do buyers usually prefer an asset purchase? First, as mentioned above, they aren't buying your company and therefore they aren't buying past problems. In an asset sale, if a customer or employee sues the company for something that happened months before the transaction, the buyer is simply part of the conduit between the plaintiff and the company. In a stock sale, the buyer owns everything and is responsible for the lawsuit.

An asset sale gives the buyer some dramatic tax advantages compared to a stock sale. Here are three common advantages:

1. The buyer can create new depreciation schedules. (Note: Both parties need to consult with their CPA or tax attorney on all of this, as there are many exceptions to every IRS rule and varying state regulations.)

2. Goodwill can be amortized over fifteen years.

3. While the noncompete agreement is considered goodwill, some of the asset allocation can go to transition training and be deductible the first year. Both are ordinary income to the seller so some of the noncompete's allocation can be shifted to training to benefit the buyer.

Real-Life Story

The seller's CPA was not experienced in transactions and asset allocation. When it came time to allocate the assets, he put $500,000 toward the noncompete agreement. I pointed out that this would be ordinary income to the seller. His first reaction was that all intangibles were goodwill so there was no difference to either buyer or seller. Upon researching it he realized his mistake. The buyer's CPA suggested reducing the total amount of the noncompete plus training to $75,000 ($50,000 to training) and received no resistance from the seller's CPA. (Consult your CPA and attorney on these matters.)

C corporation trap

The owner of a C corporation may face double taxation with an asset sale. In simple terms, the corporation may pay capital gains tax and the seller will pay tax when the proceeds are distributed to the seller personally. Therefore, sellers and their advisors will resist an asset purchase if it's a C corporation.

Buyers will generally want to discount the asset sale price if the seller insists on a stock sale. The more experienced and sophisticated the buyer and her CPA, the more likely this will occur.

One alternative to the C corporation trap

If your company is small enough (I estimate if the purchase price is under $5 million and definitely if it's under $3 million) you may be able to follow the precedent known as the Martin Ice Cream case. My clients have been involved in numerous transactions that utilized this strategy, but you should keep in mind that there are risks with everything.

In simple terms, there are two transactions. There is a sale in an amount of the seller's basis. There is also an asset sale for the amount of goodwill. It is structured as personal goodwill, and the agreement is with the seller individually, not with the corporation. The courts validated the Martin Ice Cream case (it is not part of the IRS code at the time of this writing). The seller claimed that much of the growth and profitability of the business was attributable to him and was therefore personal not corporate goodwill. The seller got one sale at a low amount, the sale of goodwill personally, and avoided double taxation. (Definitely consult your tax and legal advisors on this or any similar strategy.)

The reason I gave a maximum company and deal size above is that as a company gets larger, there is less chance the goodwill can be personally attributable to the seller versus the corporation.

Real-Life Story

On a $3 million transaction utilizing the Martin Ice Cream case precedent, I had a two-hour conference call with buyer, seller, intermediaries, and both CPAs. The CPAs, especially the buyer's, grilled the seller on his role with the company. They wanted backup justification for the personal goodwill allocation. The buyer's CPA didn't take this lightly, even though the onus was on the seller. He didn't want to be involved in a structure that couldn't be fully supported.

So why would a buyer agree to a stock sale? It could be because the seller won't consider anything else and the buyer desperately wants the business. Other reasons include the cost of an asset sale outweighing the tax advantages or contractual relationships with customers or vendors that would be violated with an asset sale.

Real-Life Story
Stu and Sherry sold a service business with hundreds of long-term leases on assets the firm rented to its customers on a short-term basis. Because they were an S corporation there was no tax disadvantage to an asset sale. However, it was a stock sale because the hassle and cost to the buyer of changing hundreds of leases, with separate vendors, far outweighed any tax savings and ran the risk of increased costs (higher rates from the vendors).

There is an old adage applicable to every type of deal (business sale, real estate, or even the sale of a piece of equipment):

It's not what you get that's important; it's what you keep.

As a business seller, don't get fixated on only the price. You have to balance the price with the terms, conditions, and taxes. Sometimes the highest price is not the best deal.

Financial Due Diligence

I am not a CPA or a CFO. However, I have worked with hundreds of clients, and together we have looked at over one thousand companies. What I am going to say here is based on those experiences: the sooner you get your CFO (in-house or outsourced) and your CPA involved, the better off you will be.

In today's world accountants typically look backward as they prepare financial statements and tax returns. CFOs and other finance people look forward and help with budgets, systems, and management reporting. Both are important, as is telling them your objective so everybody is working toward the same goal.

Here are six areas to concentrate on, based on my experience with what buyers, their advisors, and banks will be most concerned about. This summary is not meant to be all-inclusive. The larger your firm and the more complicated your business, the more scrutiny you will receive. A buyer off by 10 percent on a $1 million deal can survive a lot easier than a buyer who is off by 10 percent on a $10 million deal. Here are the top six financial due diligence areas:

1. Financial Statements
2. Financial Systems
3. Management Reports
4. Banks and Your Banker
5. Balance Sheet
6. Profits

The financial statements, systems, and reports are crucial

In-house financial statements are fine for an initial overview, but they won't mean much to a buyer or a bank doing due diligence.

Many experts advise business owners to start the exit-planning process and the preparing of the business for sale three to five years prior to the desired sell date. One of the big reasons for this lead time is related to the financial statements.

Buyers and banks will ask for three to five years of financial statements and tax returns. Anything less won't allow them to see trends and, often, going back further will not be relevant. The changes you make during your planning and preparation will manifest over this time period and be reflected in your financial statements.

Tracking what you do and when you do everything will allow you to peg activities to future financial statements and allow a buyer to see the results of your actions.

There are three basic types of accountant-prepared financial statements, and they are compiled, reviewed, and audited. A layperson's definition of each follows:

1. **Compiled statements**—Your CPA simply takes information from your accounting system and puts it together in proper format.

2. **Reviewed statements**—Your CPA reviews your statements to ensure that everything is done properly according to accounting standards. Your CPA will accept your information as true and correct.

3. **Audited statements**—Your CPA audits your books to verify revenues, costs, and everything else. The CPA may perform or assist in physical inventory and verify tangible asset values.

Consult with your CPA, other advisors, and your banker if you need audited statements, as they are very expensive. At the very least, get reviewed statements to ease the minds of the buyer and banker.

There are two ways to track revenue and expenses. You can do it on a cash basis (you record them only when received or paid) or on an accrual basis (you record revenue when billed and expenses when you are billed). Work with your CPA and you will likely realize that cash-basis accounting causes more consternation and more work for buyers and banks. They feel it is too easy to manipulate the recording of expenses or revenues and, therefore, it is easier to disguise the company's true financial position. Also, if your books are on a cash basis, when you sell, any accounts receivable (A/R) is taxed as ordinary income not capital gains (because you haven't reported it as income yet).

Cash-basis accounting can delay the recording of profit by postponing year-end deposits (to the next year) and accelerating expenses to reduce taxable income. In periods of growth, this can be a good strategy. However, if growth slows or stops it creates an inaccurate tax burden in the year of the slowdown. Cash accounting can also be used for the opposite effect. By accelerating revenues and delaying expenses, a business can show higher profits as the sale of the business gets closer. This is what scares buyers and banks.

Financial systems

While management and buyers want to see accurate financial statements as a first step to make decisions, your systems actually come before your statements. You can't have accurate statements if you don't have good systems. If no attention is paid to the accounting systems it's probably because the accuracy of the statements can be verified. If the buyer's CPA wants to investigate the systems it's probably because they question the integrity and accuracy of the statements. Keep in mind that your accounting system (QuickBooks, Peachtree, or similar) is simply the tool used.

Here are some areas to pay attention to:

- Have a meaningful chart of accounts that provides useful information. This means have the right accounts so the output can be used in a meaningful way to make decisions. If there are too few accounts then costs are lumped together and you can't easily analyze changes and variations. On the other hand, too many accounts (like the $10 million company that had 585 accounts) it's burdensome. Too much information leads to indecision.

- Have accounts in the right place so you are looking at accurate margins. For example, sales commission is often a variable cost and comes between cost of goods sold and overhead and is used to find your contribution (contribution to overhead) margin. If you lump it into overhead, it will give inaccurate budget projections. If you put it in cost of goods sold, your gross profit is misstated.

- Have proper allocations for tax purposes. One deal got hung up over the proper accounting of the overhead calculation for inventory in a manufacturing business (the CPA said a manufacturer has to allocate overhead costs to inventory and not expense those costs until the inventory is sold).

- Have a budget for at least the next twelve months. The closer past budgets are to actual results, the better. Be able to explain differences, both positive and negative.

Management reports

Work with your CFO to have meaningful management reports for your business. This allows you to know where you are, where you've been, and where you're going. A good management reporting system goes way beyond financial statements and any reports produced by QuickBooks-type systems.

When I've brought in a CFO to work with clients, they take the information from the accounting system and put it in reports that allow the management team to know what the margins truly are, what the sales pipeline is, what the sales closing rates truly are, what the true inventory turns are, and much more. These reports add value to your current operations and to the perceived overall value of your company.

My good friend Dennis Hebert, with CFO Selections in Bellevue, WA, (www.cfoselections.com), created a list of financial reporting truths to best convey that these reports are tools, they take time and effort to create, and they are not a silver-bullet solution. Here are Dennis's twelve truths:

Financial Reporting "Truths"

1. You're never done. You can always make improvements to existing reports and develop new ones.

2. Reporting is never perfect, but tends to get better with additional time, systems, and people.

3. Collecting and reporting information requires time; it's not free.

4. You'll never have all of the information you want or need.

5. Information results in dissatisfaction because it creates the desire for more information, which may not be readily available.

6. Reporting should be like peeling an onion: "big picture" summaries followed by supporting detail.

7. Numbers alone mean very little. History, goals, and industry and company knowledge are essential to bring context.

8. There is great danger in looking at short periods of time.

9. Reporting provides information for analysis and problem solving, not answers.

10. Ideally, financial reporting should reflect what is happening in your business.

11. Data that is not useful today may be useful tomorrow.

12. Favorite reporting question: "What are you going to do when you find out?"

Banks and your banker

Consult with your banker regarding her perception of the strength of your financial systems and statements. Her opinion will probably be similar to that of bankers a future buyer will consult.

If you are uncomfortable sharing that you're preparing the business for a future sale, say something like this, "I was approached by a party interested in investing in or buying my business. While I'm not interested at this time, I realize that I don't want to be in a vulnerable position if I have to sell due to an injury or illness. Also, I know that the more attractive my business is to a buyer, the better it is to me as an operator. Would you help me make sure my business looks as good as possible to your bank as if you were giving somebody an acquisition loan to buy my business?"

Balance sheet

A client who had spent most of his career as an operator managed an equity group I worked with. One thing he shared with me was that as he evaluated acquisition prospects, he had a newfound appreciation for the balance sheet compared to when he ran divisions of major companies, when he was more concerned with the bottom line.

Don't ignore your balance sheet! Work with your banker and others to make it as appealing as possible to a bank. Banks tend not to like businesses where the owner has maximized personal cash flow (at the expense of the business). A buyer will worry that there may be capital expenditures that will be his responsibility. High cash flow is great. Almost as high cash flow with a strong balance sheet is better.

Real-Life Example

Almost every deal I've been involved with recently, and almost every company I've consulted to, has needed computer system upgrades. Sometimes this is very evident and other times the importance is overlooked by the buyer or dismissed as irrelevant by the seller. Keep in mind that buyers don't acquire a company to maintain the status quo. They acquire a company because they feel they can add value and contribute to growth.

Keeping your technology up to date can come back to you in multiples when you sell. It can also provide ongoing benefits. One seller was extremely cheap on capital improvements, specifically on technology. The buyer did some upgrades, one of which was nothing more than buying a new printer. The old printer took "forever" to print reports; the accounting staff was frozen waiting for this printing. Because the new printer printed reports immediately, it noticeably increased productivity (as per the buyer). This seller was "penny wise and dollar foolish," and it cost him productivity and profits.

Profits

The previous section's emphasis on high owner cash flow should come with a caveat. It is, as mentioned before, that many owners turn their business into an extension of their personal checkbook and the company becomes a lifestyle business.

If you're a C corporation, you may be taking an extremely high salary to minimize corporate profit and corporate taxes. Smart buyers understand this and will add your salary to the profit and deduct a fair market salary for your job as company president to get a true profit figure.

S corporation owners face the opposite situation. They often take a low salary to create a high profit that flows through. The profit is taken as a distribution without paying FICA and Medicare tax on it.

If you want to sell your business for the highest possible price and get the most cash at closing (and assure the business's continuation postsale), treat the business as a business. Don't funnel personal expenses through the company, "hire" family members who don't really work for you, or do anything else that reduces profit. Show as much profit as possible for at least a few years. It will come back to you in multiples.

Real-Life Story

Here's an example of why it's important to be prepared.

The seller was forced to sell due to her spouse's terminal illness. The goal was to move from Las Vegas "back home" to the east coast so he could spend his final days with family.

She admitted she had the ultimate lifestyle business. Her personal overhead was minimal as everything, and I mean everything, was run through the business. Because this was a forced sale, due to a catastrophic event, she didn't have time to remedy this. She admitted that the amount of tax she had saved would have come back to her three to four times if she had the time to change from a lifestyle business to a business maximizing profit. This amount was mid six figures, a substantial amount for anybody.

One final note on this subject. Hiding revenues and padding expenses count equally as fraud, according to the IRS. Now the penalties may vary greatly. It could be a warning or slap on the wrist, a penalty, or criminal prosecution (criminal prosecution is primarily for not reporting revenues).

The more blatant your actions in this area, the more distrust you create with buyers. And this happens at all levels of business. One owner told us he sold his titanium scrap on the side and pocketed an unreported six figures every year. My associate and I decided not to work with him based on this and other statements that put his level of integrity in question.

Real-Life Story

Some owners, from retail to manufacturing, claim to skim cash. My comment on this is, What's worse: the owner who states his profits are really 20 percent higher because he skims cash or the owner who states his profits are 20 percent higher because he skims cash, but really he doesn't skim any cash?

Be careful in this area. Don't do it, and in any event, don't share it. Make your bottom line look as healthy as possible.

Chapter Four

Double your value: Growth strategies to get a higher price and more cash

Is your company's growth rate under 20 percent annually? Is it under 10 percent? If so, does it worry you? It should! While there's risk involved in implementing growth strategies, there's more risk in not taking any risk.

The reasons for accelerating your growth include the following:

1. Make more money

2. Increase the value of the company

3. Have dramatically more free time

Making more money and increasing your company's value go hand in hand. You can start with things like cutting expenses, but how often can you do that? Once, right? So it really comes down to this simple fact:

To increase the value of your company, you have to grow and show that continued growth is possible.

Keep in mind that growth hides a lot of operational warts! Being a hawk and monitoring expenses becomes less of an issue when you're growing the top and bottom lines. Calls from your banker become enjoyable and employees take a completely different outlook on the business and their future with the business.

What gets in the way of growth?

I like to ask audiences, "What's worse than having the capacity to make one million units annually and only selling two hundred and fifty thousand?" It's having the capacity to make two hundred and fifty thousand and selling one million. It's important to have production and sales in sync, as the following graphic shows.

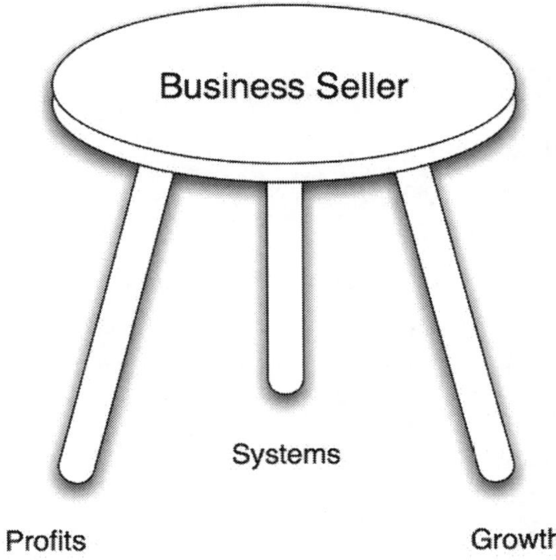

This three-legged stool of a business has been around for a long time, and it points out that every business has three main areas: operations, sales and marketing, and finance and administration. The latter lets you know if the first two are coordinating and efficient.

Here are my top seven strategies to dramatically grow your business:

1. Growth by acquisition (already covered)

2. Attitude

3. Plan

4. Implement

5. Sales

6. Finance

7. Systems

Attitude

Who sets the tone? You do! Owners and CEOs get paid to get results, and keep in mind that could mean doing nothing. Sometimes it's best to not disrupt a good thing, and when your employees' attitudes are positive, all you have to do is help them maintain it.

Let's face it, if most of your employees have a screensaver or bumper sticker that says, "A bad day (at anything) is better than a great day at work" they have the wrong attitude and you have the wrong people. You're not going to grow if your people feel their job is drudgery or they count down the seconds to five o'clock like on the TV show *The Office*.

When I give talks to audiences of business owners, I ask them to rate themselves (one to ten, ten being great) on the following three statements:

1. New ideas are implemented successfully and on time.

2. I know exactly how to motivate and get the most out of my key people.

3. My company, its culture, and my employees are poised for growth.

(A complete list of all rating questions like these is in Appendix C.)

New ideas are implemented successfully and on time.

I heard from a national consulting firm and a Seattle firm with dozens of small business clients that the number-one reason growth targets aren't met is inadequate implementation. Too often this means the owner and the top staff are getting bogged down in the day to day. It's tough, but it's absolutely necessary to delegate and teach your management team to delegate.

Often the reason is trying to do too much. Too many people, business owners included, are great at starting projects, and then starting more projects, and then even more, until there's too much going on and nothing getting finished. Follow the advice given for implementing a marketing plan: Take two of your twenty ideas, get going on them, perfect the process, and then, and only then, move on to your third idea.

Real-Life Story

The employees said that the owner was the top reason things didn't get done in the fifty-person firm. He had a habit of doing too much, getting involved in all decisions, and procrastinating. I got him to remove things from his desk (and inbox) by having him ask himself, "Is this below my pay grade?" If it was, it went to somebody else.

This started working and working great. Then he told me his management team was overwhelmed with all he was passing off on them. So, it was time to get the management team to learn to delegate. This required hiring a new employee or two, but as business was "great" this was necessary anyway.

I know exactly how to motivate and get the most out of my key people.

Talk about a never-ending subject. Almost every business publication has regular columns or frequent articles on managing and leading people. Call it culture, team building, or anything else, but it's the same issue over and over at almost every company. Here are three tips for getting people to work together better, assume responsibility, and increase productivity:

1. Don't be a controlling owner; most employees want to grow, learn, and advance in their careers. Let them. Responsibility comes with experience and leads to better results.

2. Let people stumble and fall. You need to be there with the safety net, but there's nothing wrong with letting good people learn from experience, as we all have learned. This doesn't mean that you put a rookie in charge of your number-one customer; it means providing small responsibilities, one small step at a time, and monitoring progress.

3. As stated multiple times in this book, let go. Delegate anything below your pay grade. In other words, don't do anything someone else can do (almost) as well as you can.

This is not easy. If it was, anybody could run a business, and we know that's not anywhere close to true.

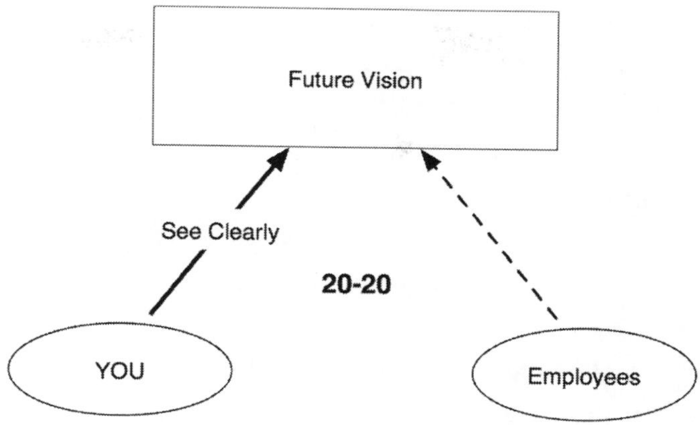

My company, its culture, and my employees are poised for growth.

Daniel Pink, in his book *Drive*, quotes an owner about his employees: "They're not resources, they're partners." Here are my top three factors:

- Employees want to see their ideas at least considered, if not accepted.

- They want to feel a sense of accomplishment, understand their value, and be part of a winning team.

- Partners work toward a common goal.

Plan

Question: What's the difference in the growth rates of companies that have a business plan compared to companies that don't have a plan? While you can probably find a variety of answers on the Internet, the one I like to quote is from one of the large accounting firms, and it states that companies with a plan grow sales and profits at double the rate of those without a plan.

Strategy is the "what," tactics are the "how," and they have to work together. For most of you, any plan has an emphasis on sales and marketing. Most of the rest, as pictured in the three-legged stool above, is important, but revenue growth should be your top consideration.

Marketing—Marketing is anything you do to get your name in front of prospective customers and people who can refer customers to you. There are a wide variety of tactics, including advertising, blogs, sponsorships, social media, speaking (at trade shows, for example), writing technical articles, and a lot more. Know what works and what doesn't in your industry and get the word out.

Money, a budget, and cash flow projections are a good place to start. Remember, it takes cash to grow a business. That cash may be used to hire people or buy more equipment or it may get sucked into higher accounts receivable and inventory. An integral part of any growth planning process is to know the cash it will take. Have good accounting systems and management reports.

Management structure—The next chapter has a sample organization (org) chart. If you don't have one, make it part of your plan. Know who does what, who they report to, and so on. It allows you, and others, to delegate and gives employees a clear understanding of who their boss is. A confused employee will be an unproductive employee.

A buyer is much more comfortable paying a price on the high end of the fair range when there's a team in place and the role of the owner is reduced. Or, let's say the role of the owner is elevated to where she spends the majority of her time on strategy, vision, and growth.

To summarize the above section on planning, it's important that part of your planning process be the setting of goals. Know where you want to be, both financially and nonfinancially. Do you want sales to grow by 18 percent next year? Is it important to take two weeks more vacation or be out of the office by five o'clock at least three days per week? What about helping your people grow into new roles? Incorporate all of these categories into your master plan and share them with your management team. Keep in mind that your goals are your strategy and vision. Make them reachable, but a stretch.

Also make sure your plan covers the final four growth strategies: systems, implement, sales and finance.

Real-Life Story

The owner, the owner's spouse, and the COO all gave the accounting staff direction. The problem was that none of them understood finance or accounting very well. Compounding the problem was that the accounting department was not qualified enough for the size to which the company had grown so nobody would stand up to management (out of both fear and being unsure).

This was a three-pronged problem. There was inadequate structure and delegating systems, they had not hired the right people for the job, and because of these two factors they also had inadequate financial systems so the accuracy of the financial reports was suspect.

Implement (the right way)

A few pages ago I mentioned how growth is often stymied by the lack of implementation. The ideas are there, they just never get acted on.

When implementing, pay attention to the right details, and the first detail on the list is time management. If you don't block out time, for your team and yourself, to work on implementing your growth plans, how are you going to grow? Prioritizing growth, and having your team allocate all the necessary resources, is a must.

Realize the first thing almost all your people are going to say is, "We don't have time for this." They do, and you know it. Too many people fill their days with routine tasks instead of things that are important. Delegate and get them to do it.

Details come in many varieties and I won't be presumptuous and try to tell you what particular details are important to your business and you. Start by paying attention to the items in the other sections in this chapter and your nonfinancial factors (below) and apply the nuances specific to your company. Do so and you'll do fine.

Think of this like a fishing trip. Good fishers know the right place to fish, the right time to go, the proper bait to use, the depth to fish, and a lot more. It's what allows them to catch more fish than I do.

A cousin of mine goes salmon fishing on Lake Michigan. He told me that he's on the lake thirty minutes before sunrise and done fishing two hours after the sun is up. Because anything after that is boating, not fishing.

Real-Life Story

When I was eleven years old, my parents bought a lake cabin. As we started going there, a neighbor took an interest in us and guided us through some of the ins and outs of the area and the lake.

Harry was recently retired and his wife and he had built a house on the lake so they could live there six months a year. It's an understatement to say he was a good fisher. I can still remember when he would take us to our lake's "hot spots." Three of us would be in our boat and he'd be ten yards away in his boat. After sixty to ninety minutes, we'd have a couple fish between us and he'd have a stringer full. I'm sure if one of us had sat in his boat the results wouldn't have changed.

It's not only important to pay attention to the details—you have to recognize them first. A buyer will want to know those little secrets because that's what's created goodwill and why the price for your business will see based on profits not net asset value.

A mystery I read years ago had the detective saying, "It's in the details; it's always in the details." Think about going to a sporting event, the theater, or a concert. The athletes, actors, and musicians practice the little things over and over so that when they hit their stage it comes together as a successful performance. You have to do the same in your business.

Work on your nonfinancial factors—the value of your business is based on them. Remember, financial statements are historical snapshots of points in time. The nonfinancial factors let you (and a buyer) know the likelihood of profits continuing. They include, but are not limited to, the following, and there's much more on them later:

- Customers
- Employees
- Vendors
- Competition
- Technology
- Space (size, lease term, rent amount)
- Financing (ability)
- Marketing

Follow-through is the most important detail. You can have the best strategy and design the best tactics, but if you don't implement correctly and with speed, you will lose ground because the chances are your competitors aren't sitting back letting you dawdle on your plans. They're racing forward.

Real-Life Story

Dick was an operations guy (and good with customers) while Kathie was a CFO by experience. They said having adequate management meant they could both do some planning in addition to their daily responsibilities. Their benefits from this commitment to planning included the following:

- ***Faster growth***
- ***Increased profit***
- ***A higher salary***
- ***Increased local market share***
- ***A growing national client base***

As an outside observer, there is no doubt in my mind that the key to their business taking off like a rocket was the devotion to planning and implementing systems (emphasis on implementing). Having management skills is one thing; using them is another. This means not filling the day with tasks other employees can easily do (this is mentioned three times in this chapter because it's so important).

Let's look at examples of handling the details. Keep in mind, they may sound simple, but they work. Like a lot of things in business and life, it's best to follow Occam's Razor, which states that the best solution is usually the one with the fewest assumptions. This means keep it simple and don't overthink these things, as the following Real-Life Story demonstrates.

Real-Life Story

My client was preparing for her annual wholesale-only weekend sale. As we discussed the marketing efforts, I took it all in and said something like, "You're missing the most important thing."

Fast forward about a month and I get an early Monday-morning call from her. She starts out by thanking me profusely because the sale was five times larger than any previous sale. When I asked why she was thanking me, her response was that it was my marketing input that caused this—she knew, they asked people what drove them to attend.

What was this idea that spurred the huge turnout? Make a follow-up call to the invitees the week prior to the sale. Simple, but incredibly effective.

Sales

Sales are what happen after marketing, although sometimes a good old-fashioned cold call works (however, it's better if marketing has produced name recognition). In your plan, address your sales strategy, tactics, people needed, and so on. Sales just don't happen. In his classic sales book, *How to Master the Art of Selling*, Tom Hopkins writes, "… selling is the highest paid hard work—and the lowest paid easy work—that I could find."

As a business owner seeking to grow, you need to weed out those who want easy work, like a new hire in the first sales job I had. This employee's goal was to make enough money to go fishing as often as possible. Think he was ever in the office early or late in the day or on weekends?

Real-Life Story
A client told me that his sales team had a handful of outside salespeople making $125 to 150,000 annually and another handful making $30 to 50,000. The big difference was that the high earners got out and prospected, saw customers, and had high activity. The low earners were seen around the office a lot. His strategy was to make the low earners inside salespeople and hire more people who would develop business.

This is where it gets fun. You have to like (love) sales to achieve growth in a small business. My postcollege career started off with me on the buying side. Salespeople were calling on me. My life after that has been 180 degrees different, whether you call it pure sales, business development, or generating consulting clients, I'm on the other side of the table. It took a bit of learning—I'm not a corporate sales expert or trainer but I have helped companies, including my own, grow, and it often comes down to the sales effort.

A sales manager way back when taught me to, at the end of the day, "always make one more call." This means that by the end of the year each salesperson has had 250 more contacts than they would otherwise have had. It doesn't matter if these are new contacts, relationship building, follow-up calls on proposals, or any other kind. An extra 250 contacts will generate more business, assuming the person making the contacts isn't completely incompetent (that has to do with hiring though, doesn't it?).

So what's going on if you can't grow, can't generate more sales, are stuck on a plateau, or similar? Let's look at three top reasons:

1. Your value proposition isn't adequate for the current market. Here's an example we regularly read or hear about. Microsoft can't get any traction in the smartphone market. The iPhone changed the game in 2007 and Google's Android operating

system opened the market up to the masses. Microsoft was late to the game, and as I write this, even though its phones get great reviews, its value proposition with the customers is lacking and, therefore, stagnant.

2. Your salespeople aren't making enough calls or are falling into the trap of hiding behind e-mails and thinking it's a legitimate customer contact. Low activity is a killer, as mentioned previously.

3. Your salespeople aren't very good. If your salespeople won't make calls, can't get appointments, or can't get orders, replace them. Is it harsh? Yes, mainly to you and your bottom line. Is it easy to get a good replacement? Not usually. In fact, I'd say that the reason I hear the most for why a mediocre salesperson is kept on is the cost and risk associated with hiring a replacement. So ordinary performance is tolerated. If you won't or can't replace poor performers, you better figure out a way to make them better.

What it comes down to is your people, and maybe you, have to realize it's a numbers game and you must take action. This means implement your plan, know your objectives and metrics, and be able to adjust during the process (isn't that what sales meetings are for?).

Real-Life Story

Tell me what's wrong with this picture. It's from a client who shall remain nameless. He owns a good business and the profits are in the $300 to 500,000 range, in spite of what follows, which came directly from the owner:

- ***There are no sales goals.***

- ***There are no written job descriptions.***

- ***There is a new person doing outside sales to generate new customers (without goals or a job description).***

- ***The most experienced salesperson is underperforming, has been for at least two years, and yet the owner has not had a "tough talk" with him.***

- ***There is no incentive program.***

This is quite common in small business. You may relate to it. Just think how the business could grow if this owner did some of the things you've deduced could be done to grow his business.

Here's a simple outline for successful sales. As "the devil is in the details," I can't discuss any industry specifics, just generalities:

- Prospect and stay in touch.

- Build and maintain relationships.

- Ask questions to qualify.

- Find the objective, also known as the problem to solve.

- Confirm with the prospect that you're in agreement on the objective, what's involved, a tentative budget, and so on.

- If needed, put together a quote, proposal, or summary of the work.

- If not needed, suggest a solution right away.

- Follow up, show interest, and provide value without being asked (especially after an order is received).

In my first sales-related job I was sent to a weeklong training session where I learned, from a Wilson Learning course, the four reasons people don't buy. These are timeless, I don't know who created them, and they make 100 percent sense to me:

1. **No need**—Calling on an aerospace manufacturer to sell agricultural products, obviously no need. You get the point; not everybody is a prospect so good research is important.

2. **No hurry**—"We have a potential problem, but other things are ahead of it." This could mean they have a year's worth of supplies, they know their roof is on its last legs but it has a couple more years, or the forklift sputters a bit but it's not worth worrying about until it dies.

3. **No money**—They love you and what you have but they're struggling. Believe me, there is usually always money or financing if your perceived value is high enough.

4. **No trust**—This is often the real reason. While the above can be real reasons, they're also used as excuses when prospects don't trust you or feel your product isn't the solution. Here's an example from my world. The head of an investment fund had made an offer on a business to buy, we're in due diligence, there's a couple issues, and the tipping point to pull the offer was when he said to me, "The bottom line is, I just don't trust one of the sellers." My answer was that his decision was made; you can't do a deal if full trust isn't there.

Finance

Too many owners love their product or the customer relationships and ignore the numbers. Finance is the third leg of the business stool. As I was taught, it tells you if sales and operations are in sync.

In chapter three I presented my friend Dennis Hebert's "Financial Reporting Truths." These management reports break down information so it's usable. They are not a panacea, you still need your experience and smarts to make the right decisions, but you're now putting the odds more in your favor.

Real-Life Story

First, let's point out a fallacy many people have about business operations. I hear all the time something like, "You can put in a general manager to run the business and pay him $100,000 a year (for this $10 million business)." The point of this is that brokers and owners are trying to minimize the value of the owner and artificially increase the price of the business.

Gary is a perfect example of why the above is a fallacy and ties into having the right numbers and reports.

Gary owned what might be called a cash-generating machine. He maybe worked half a day, primarily doing the non-A/R and A/P accounting, took numerous vacations including to his condo in Central America, and one would say he was a partially absentee owner.

However, Gary had been at it for so long that he could walk in, gaze around, look at some numbers, and know from experience if things were going right or if they were off kilter. Do you have that ability? Will it be so easy if you double or triple in size? Most importantly, how long will it take a buyer to get to that point?

> ***The importance of management reports, and paying attention to the numbers, is so you get out of the "unconscious competent" mode and build a business where the systems allow others, your management team and buyer, to make the same smart decisions you easily make.***

Every business is different, so I will keep the following brief and somewhat generic. You can use reports and financial information to answer these questions:

- Are individual lines of business profitable?
- Are different markets and locations profitable?
- Is your tracking of sales activity correct?
- Are your salespeople getting positive results?
- How effective is your marketing activity?
- Do you have an accurate sales (or order) pipeline?
- What is your success rate on proposals or bids by type of job, proposal, writer, and more?

The biggest mistake in this area is when an owner thinks because she has accounting software she also has accurate and meaningful information. The old computer adage applies to accounting also: garbage in, garbage out. If your chart of accounts isn't accurate and consistent, you can't accurately compare one time period to another. Even if it is accurate and consistent, accounting software usually just gives raw data. You want it in a meaningful format. And, by the way, when the reports are put into Excel it's easy to create pictures and graphs that showcase results and trends in a format all can understand.

> *Real-Life Story*
>
> ***As of 2014 (and I'm sure it won't get any easier in the future), the SBA is requiring banks and business appraisers to justify and document all "add-backs." Add-backs are expenses the business deducted that the seller claims aren't really necessary business expenses. This often includes personal travel, family vehicles, life insurance and more. Here's what a buyer recently wrote to a seller about a list of add-backs that were used to adjust the price (luckily in this case they were small and simple):***
>
> ***"The analyst is looking for 'documentation' of expenditures on the above items over the last three years."***
>
> ***As one banker explained to me, "We're an approved government program lender. It's hard to justify owners saying they cheated the government (by deducting personal expenses) and then want the benefit of a government-guaranteed loan."***

Systems

The word "systems" is scary to many business owners. They think process management as done by Ford, Boeing, GE, and others and insist that's one reason they like having their own business: so they have freedom, flexibility, and independence.

Systems are simply a way of doing things the same way every time in a manner that works. It takes out the "winging it," lets employees know management's expectations, and improves productivity and cash flow. You're using a lot of systems right now, even if you don't think you are. You have a system for how mail is handled, bills paid, orders shipped, and more. Just apply this to all aspects of your business, especially sales, and growth will increase.

Here's what systems really are: the replication and documentation of things you routinely do. You probably do a lot of it already; it's just not documented as well as it should be. We know you do it in your accounting department, at least to some extent.

Your goal should be that a new employee, manager, or a buyer can walk in and quickly learn the intricacies of the job (or, for a buyer, of the business). The story below demonstrates how simple a system can be. Salespeople, the good ones anyway, have their proven process. Every job should have one.

Think franchising; it's all about reproducible systems. Every franchise out there was created because someone created a way of doing business that others could successfully replicate. Heck, McDonald's made its way by figuring out how high school and college kids could deliver a consistent product that met the company's and customers' expectations.

Don't let it be overwhelming. Simply document what worked, what didn't, and why. Get all employees to do the same. It will accelerate growth and impress buyers.

Real-Life Story

Here's a very simple system we put in for a remodeling contracting business that had severe cash flow issues. The business specialized in insurance claim work and this created some urgency because when your house is damaged or flooded, you want it fixed ASAP.

The owner of the business thought that urgency meant starting jobs ASAP. He was wrong: it meant finishing jobs ASAP. The company's problem was that by starting too many jobs the workers were spread too thin and they spent way too much time traveling from job to job and back and forth from suppliers.

Here's the simplified version of the system we put in place. The customers were told the job would be put in the queue when the following conditions had been met:

1. ***The customer had chosen all of the materials (this could be colors, hardware design, door and window styles, etc.).***

2. ***A deposit was received.***

3. ***All materials were delivered to the site.***

Not complicated, is it? Amazing how this solved production and cash flow problems.

Larger businesses sell for more than smaller ones, all things being equal. Growing businesses with a high likelihood of continued growth sell for more than flat, stagnant businesses. Don't be fooled, growth is not always easy, but it is achievable if you put in the effort, follow a plan, implement, and execute correctly by paying attention to the details. The results will benefit you now and when you exit.

Chapter Five

What do you really have?

If you perform due diligence on your business, as a buyer would, you will find that improvement naturally follows. If you bought your business, or grew by acquisition, you know this. Buyers get excited when they see areas in a company where they can add value. Your goal is to uncover areas you and your team can add value as you prepare for a future exit so that you can sell for a higher price, with more cash at closing and less hassle, because the buyer sees opportunity and the structure in place to achieve that opportunity.

Business buyers are an inquisitive lot (and should be). There's an old saying, "When I ask you what time it is, don't tell me how to build the watch." Buyers are the opposite; they want to know how to build the watch, in this case, all the little things that make your business special and worth buying at a price you find acceptable. In other words, they want to know about all of the things that give you a competitive advantage.

The subjects in this chapter are the heart and soul of your business. Financial statements show where your company was at a particular time in history. The nonfinancial factors paint a picture of where the company's going, whether you're likely to meet your projections, and what risks are lurking under the surface of your financial statements.

You (and other owners)

If there are multiple owners, get that information to a buyer early in the process. Make sure the other owners are onboard with the plan to sell the company. In chapter one I discussed the reasons why owners sell. You need to be able to articulate this reason, especially if you don't have health reasons, aren't of retirement age, or don't have another reason that automatically makes sense to a buyer.

Know what you want to do postsale. There is normally a transition period that you provide to the buyer as part of the purchase of your goodwill. This is normally sixty days to six months depending on the nature and complication factor of the business. After transition, do you want to be a consultant, an employee, or an independent sales rep? Would this be full time or part time? Do you want to walk away and not be involved?

Know what you want and at the same time realize that more than 90 percent of the time the buyer wants you gone. He wants to be the person in charge and doesn't want somebody looking over his shoulder saying, "We've always done it differently." Your staying on can also create dysfunction with the employees. Employees sometimes play the old boss against the new boss, like teenagers playing Mom and Dad against each other.

Finally, if you have any other business interests, especially if they relate to this company, get it out sooner rather than later. This could be another business you own that shares expenses, uses employees, or shares facilities. This could also be partial ownership you have in a customer or vendor business (rare, but it happens).

Your business

The more inquisitive the buyer is, the better (especially once you have a signed letter of intent outlining price and terms). The best buyers, who become the best owners, are inquisitive and want to understand the intricacies that make the business what it is.

Craft a good answer for the question "What value do you provide your customers?"

Fill in the buyer on the importance of what you do. This is your value proposition, and it creates your competitive advantage. Remember, you grow by leveraging your competitive advantage, so pay close attention to this.

Go into detail about your main products or services (from now on I will use the term *product* to cover products, services, or a combination of the two). As you cover the potential for each, don't be afraid to discuss the risks certain products may face. Nobody, especially a business buyer, will believe that all is wonderful all the time.

Weave company insights into the conversation before the buyer asks about them. Remember, buyers buy because they like the direction of the business. History is important (and the basis for the business's value) and yet a great history without a bright future means an unsalable business (or salable at a fire-sale price).

The ability to grow your product line is important. Whether it's a driving issue or not to you, it will be to a buyer; so be able to articulate product expansion. Do you have an in-house engineering or creative department? Is it market driven? Will new products come from acquiring another company? It's not just the answers that are important, it is also the fact that you have done your homework and have a handle on the strategies required.

At the same time, mention any limitations. This could be license agreements, copyrights, patents, tariffs, or royalties (due the owner of intellectual property). Again, having a handle on the issue is as or more important than the answer.

Every company has intellectual property, although we tend to think of it in terms of things like patents, software code, and the like. A basic machine shop has a way of doing things that pleases customers. So does an auto repair facility, a nursing home, and a restaurant. My point is that you have intangibles, whether copyrighted or patented or not, and that is part of your competitive advantage.

Ownership structure

An organizational chart, also known as an org chart, could go in the section on employees and management. I'm putting it here because to a buyer the org chart is as much a part of the big picture as it is the daily operations. It's not hard to create one. Microsoft Word and Excel have templates that make it easy.

The purpose of an org chart is to show responsibilities and relationships. This chart should show all the departments of your company. Not just for now, but for where you want to be. For example, the following simple example shows a company with three basic divisions under the owner. I've not added levels under operations or finance and administration, but there definitely would be a structure there also.

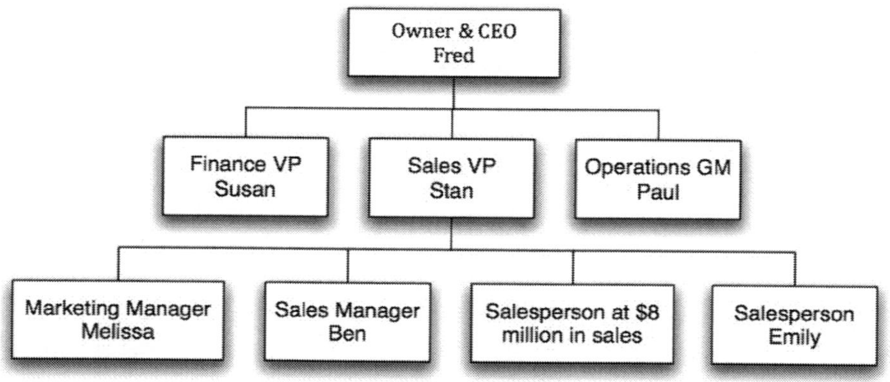

The above example is simplistic. Rather than detail everybody in this sample firm, I want to make the point that as you plan, you will have positions that are unfilled. In this example, the company is projecting it will need another salesperson when sales hit $8 million annually. It's this type of forethought that will impress buyers and make them want to pay more for your business.

A long time ago I read that a good strategy for an org chart is to have a box for everything that gets done in the business. If you have twenty employees and thirty-five tasks (boxes on the chart) it's OK. Some people will be in multiple boxes. The smaller the business is, the more likelihood of this. In fact, with a young and growing company, the owner's name will be in a lot of boxes. Your job, whether you have five, fifty, or five hundred employees, is to remove your name from as many boxes as possible. This adds great value to your firm.

Buyers and banks will want to see a list of owners (if more than one) and board members. Do you have woman-minority status, which means if it's a women and/or minority owned business you will be able to fill mandated quotas on public works projects (which must do their best to hire women-minority owned companies)? If you are male, is your wife a co-owner to get the woman-minority status? That may be an issue when selling. Be prepared for the question about the effect of a male or nonminority owner if the buyer can't get that status.

What are the intricacies that make your company what it is?

People—This has to do with requirements, not capabilities. While not a pressing issue, buyers will want to know if you have a human resources policy and if you are current on all regulatory matters for your size firm. An employee policies and procedures manual is something you should have, to a varying degree based on size. (At the end of chapter seven there is a guest essay from an HR outsourcing firm owner that expands on this subject.)

Have you articulated your vacation and sick-pay policy? Are these policies competitive or rich? Do you allow carryover of vacation from year to year? If you're a union shop, be able to state the advantages of being union (because many buyers have nonunion as one of their top criteria).

Real-Life Story

Ray was selling his business and the subject of vacations and sick leave came up. Ray was seventy years old and truly coasting. He simply wanted to keep everybody happy and thus had an extremely generous vacation policy with 100 percent rollover.

When the buyer investigated this area, he was shocked because most of the employees had been using about 50 percent of their vacation time for years and had stockpiled months of vacation. Of course, this was not on the balance sheet.

It cost Ray about $100,000 to pay for this vacation time. It took the buyer almost no time to consult with an HR professional and implement a new realistic vacation policy with a "use it or lose it" clause.

Who does what—Technically, this is part of human resources. You should have job descriptions for each employee, employee bios, and any performance reviews. Buyers want to know if the current employees and management are capable of driving future growth.

Benefits—We don't know what our politicians are going to do, so it's smart to have a reasonable benefit plan that is compliant. Do you have a retirement plan, and if not, why not? Individual buyers coming out of the corporate world are used to good benefit and retirement plans. Larger companies have these plans and will adjust your profit downward if they have to add benefit plan costs.

One issue that can become sticky is an annual bonus program. Sellers look at bonus plans as optional compensation. Once given and continued from year to year, employees consider it part of their expected compensation. I've heard sellers say that the annual bonus is really profit (on which to base the price) because the bonuses don't have to be given. Pretend you are buying a company. Would you want one of your first decisions to be not paying the year-end bonus?

Insurance—Compile a list of all your insurance coverage, especially those that are mandated, your agents, the annual cost of each, and the last time you reviewed your policies. Insurance needs are constantly changing. Disaster planning is coming into vogue and part of it involves insurance.

Intellectual property—Make sure all your trademarks, copyrights, and similar are properly registered and displayed. If you have or grant any license agreements, have them in order and current. The same goes for any incoming or outgoing royalties.

Accounts and assets—Have a list of all assets that require titles, have liens, and so on. Also have a list of all accounts that will need to be changed. This includes, but is not limited to, utilities, Internet hosting, cell phones, janitorial, copier, FedEx, and the post office.

If you have any off–balance-sheet items, such as copier leases, Yellow Pages advertising, or any vehicle or equipment leases, get that information to the buyer sooner than later.

Government regulations—If you even think you need licenses or permits or have a hazardous-materials issue, make sure you are compliant. Does the government require at least one employee to have a certification (for example, in Washington State any company providing low- or high-voltage electrical services must have a licensed administrator on staff)?

Record keeping—Do you have any other record-keeping systems? This could be for personnel, production, quality assurance, complaints, or tracking marketing efforts. How is this documented? How often to you produce these reports (and your financial statements)? Is it timely information that provides value?

Litigation—Has the business ever been involved in a lawsuit? If so, what was the nature and outcome of each major case? Describe legal action that you think might be threatened or pending against the company.

Capital expenditures—Depreciation (of assets) is technically a noncash accounting item that applies to deducting capital expenditures for tax purposes. It is much more important to know what amount of annual capital spending is required to allow the business to remain competitive. With ever-changing tax laws, this is the number a buyer should focus on—not what you wrote off or when you wrote it off, but what the buyer will need to spend the first year or two.

Chapter Six

Value: It's more than the financial statements

Business buyers often overlook the importance of the nonfinancial factors. However, every buyer will want to know about your customers. In fact, a bank recently had questions about the seller's customers on its loan due diligence checklist.

The point of this book is to help you make your business as attractive as possible to buyers so they will pay the high end of the fair market price range. There is no better place to concentrate your efforts than with customers. What you do here spills over and makes your employees look better and become more productive, makes your margins better, and creates the image of a partnership (with the customers) that will impress buyers.

Financial statements are only 20% of your analysis

At "Partner" On-Call Network we use the acronym CELBS to represent the nonfinancial factors. CELBS stands for the following:

- Customers

- Employees
- Landlord
- Banker
- Suppliers
- And any other nonfinancial factors that affect the business and its future profitability

Buyers will usually start with questions about customer concentration and loyalty and the competence of the key employees and management. The more sophisticated the buyer, the sooner she will ask about other factors and the deeper she will go.

Your customers

The first factor buyers and banks will ask about is customer concentration. No matter what your rationale, the higher the concentration of sales, the bigger the red flag. A business with 60 percent of sales spread out over sixty customers has a lot less risk than a business with 60 percent of sales concentrated with just three customers.

You likely know who your top customers are, the relationship you have with them, and their percentage of annual sales. If you have customers doing more than 10 percent of your annual sales, it's time to concentrate on diversifying your customer base. This may require growing while keeping your top customers at the same level (lowering their percentage of sales).

Don't dismiss this as irrelevant because they "love" you. Love can be fickle. Your goal should be no customer accounting for more than 5 percent of sales. This does not apply only to end-users. Having thousands of end users being serviced by a handful of distributors or reps is the same as having a handful of customers.

Real-Life Story

George was selling his manufacturers' rep firm to his key salesperson. On first look, the customer concentration was horrible. The top customer accounted for 25 to 30 percent of sales. However, upon further analysis I noticed that it was a different top customer every year. On a three-year average, no customer accounted for more than 10 percent of sales. If you have a situation similar to this, be sure to look at the long-term picture; don't focus only on one year, and have a good explanation on why this is so.

So, who are your firm's customers and what are the trends in this customer group? Why do they buy from you at a price that allows you to make a profit? This is your competitive advantage. I suggest you take some time now and write down answers to this question, even if it's part of your business or sales plan. Your answer here is almost as important as your answer to the question "Why are you selling?"

Why do your customers buy from you? What are their top considerations?

- Price
- Quality
- Service
- Availability
- Sales
- Engineering

- Credit term
- Right of return
- Technology

Real-Life Example

There's an old business adage that says: "We can offer the best in price, quality, or service. Take two of the three. It's impossible to offer all three and stay in business." It's true—if customers (or you with your suppliers) want the best quality and the best service, you have to pay for it.

Many years ago we took our kids to Venice Beach while in the Los Angeles area for a baseball tournament. Everybody got T-shirts, cheap T-shirts (like three for $10). After a handful of times through the washing machine, we found out why they were so cheap. You get what you pay for.

Customer concentration

Business is constantly moving and changing. A previous example explained how every year one company had a top customer that accounted for too high a percentage of sales, but it was never the same top customer. Concentration is where all customer due diligence will start. Every buyer will want to know this, and fairly soon in the process.

Here's a tip: Once you have a signed nondisclosure agreement and the buyer asks for a customer list, provide the list, showing annual sales volumes *without* the customer names. Only show a list with customers' names after you have signed a letter of intent with an agreed-upon price and terms.

What are the red flags to a buyer and a bank? Any customer over 10 percent is considered a red flag. In some cases it could be 5 percent, especially if there is industry concentration (more on this shortly). Statistics from the Risk Management Association (RMA), the IRS, and an old article in *Inc.* magazine state that the average profit for small businesses is 7 to 10 percent. Lose a customer that is 12 percent of your business, and assuming you have a 50 percent gross profit margin, that 7 to 10 percent bottom line just turned into 1 to 4 percent. You may survive and bring it back, but what about a buyer with acquisition debt payments? This creates a negative cash flow position, the bank is worried, and the buyer's risk just multiplied.

What should you expect if you have high customer concentration? If your buyer has an experienced acquisition advisor or a transaction-experienced attorney, you should expect some type of erosion clause. In simple terms, an erosion clause will state that if certain (named) customers stop doing business with the company with no fault to the buyer (for example, the customer is purchased and the acquiring company has its own trusted supplier), the price is reduced, payments to you are delayed, or some other action is taken based on your situation.

As a seller, you will be thinking about how hard it is to prove that losing a customer was not a result of the buyer's actions; this is a very legitimate thought. There are three answers to this:

1. Get yourself out of this situation by reducing your customer concentration.

2. If you think the buyer can't handle the business and its customer relationships, don't sell to that particular buyer.

3. Put in monitoring clauses for you to be actively checking on the business and its customer relationships.

Real-Life Story
I received a call from a desperate owner I wish I could have helped. His firm, doing about $10 million in annual sales, needed an investment ASAP, as it was about to close its doors. He was a specialty subcontractor in the health food and supplement industry with one customer accounting for about 60 percent of annual sales.

The two companies had grown together. He told me the customer started with him and did $100,000 of business the first year. He felt a certain loyalty to this customer and thought it was reciprocal. It was reciprocal until the customer hired a new CEO who had a friend with a competing manufacturing operation. They changed vendors almost immediately, leading to this owner's desperation.

One area often overlooked is industry concentration. While not as important as customer diversification, it is wise to sell into numerous, and as diverse as possible, industries. Industries can have wild swings. We all saw this with construction starting in 2008, and it surprised a lot of people.

I worked on two deals in 2006 that were related to commercial construction. All research, done by buyers and sellers, indicated that commercial construction in Seattle would be strong for at least five years. We all know what happened. If you can show industry diversification, and how you achieved it, the perception of your business's quality will improve.

Customer satisfaction

Do you have any major customers that have left over the last two years? If so, why did they leave? If you were buying your business, would you be satisfied with this answer?

The best way to determine how happy your customers are is to have a third party do some research. It could be as simple as calling as a reference check or conducting a customer satisfaction survey. Don't have your people do it. Don't do it yourself. When a buyer does this it is a third party. Depending on your business, you may add to the usual topics I concentrate on:

- Product
- Service
- Support
- Delivery
- Timeliness
- Admin (billing and ordering)
- Employeesv

I ask customers to rank each category on a one-to-ten scale and then follow up by asking what the company can do better, if there are any other services they would like to see offered, and if there is anything upcoming that will cause them to not do business at the same level or greater. You can add other categories specific to your industry. The bottom line is to determine where you shine and where you don't (as much as you would like to).

Selling process

Buyers will be mildly interested in how you sell (mildly compared to their interest in concentration and satisfaction). Often this comes down to the fit between buyer and seller. If you have a sales organization and the owner needs to understand sales, sales management, and motivation, you are probably not going to sell to an industrial engineer.

Real-Life Story

My client had a convoluted sales compensation plan. The salespeople received a low base salary and bonuses (really a commission) when their monthly sales exceeded a benchmark amount. However, the bonuses kicked in before the company covered its base costs of employment.

For example, if it took $50,000 of monthly sales per person to cover employment costs, including salary, benefits, share of overhead, and a target profit, the bonus started at $40,000. This meant the company was losing money on each salesperson unless that person's sales greatly exceeded $50,000.

One, of many, things we did was to redesign the compensation plan so the salespeople covered their total costs before getting a bonus.

More important is the selling process, sales cycle, and closing ratio. The latter is often the most important. Management reports and sales is a natural place to make sure you have a good reporting system.

To help the sales manager who, like in many small businesses, was a great salesperson, the most qualified to be sales manager, but not experienced or skilled in management, we tracked the following:

1. Prospects into the system (call-in, referral, repeat)

2. Prospects who agreed to meet (after calling in)

3. Prospects with a legitimate need who requested a proposal

4. Proposals presented

5. Successful closes

Know these statistics; be able to present them to a buyer and demonstrate how you've improved your closing ratio, and your credibility will increase and potential buyers will respect you.

If you have contracts with your customers, make sure they stay in force if you sell the company. This can be a sticky issue. It could affect the structure of your sale (asset versus stock) and what a buyer is willing to pay.

A sales consultant recently shared with me that his clients are scared when one or two top salespeople control the vast majority of the company's relationships and sales. Salesperson concentration can be almost as large an issue as customer concentration. This is a dependency and one that, if present, needs to be fixed.

A business buyer may feel that it's worse if those customer relationships are with the seller (versus the sales staff). The buyer knows the seller will be gone in ninety days. At least with the salespeople he knows they will want to keep their jobs and hope the buyer injects a spark of enthusiasm to grow the company (and their compensation).

When you, the owner, control and have very tight relationships with the customers, you have created personal goodwill. You want the customers thinking of the company first, not any individual, as this creates company goodwill, which is much easier to transfer to a buyer (who will pay more for it).

Vendors

A lot of attention is paid to customer concentration. Equal attention should be paid to supplier concentration, supplier innovation, and the health of the suppliers' companies.

A banker shared with me that her bank almost didn't make a loan because the borrower was dependent on one key supplier. The bank finally did some due diligence on the supplier, determined it was solid, and made the loan.

Even if you are just starting to think of an exit, start paying attention to all of your suppliers and be prepared to explain why this is not a risk area.

Real-Life Story

A former client invited me to lunch and shared that his top manufacturer, accounting for 60 percent of his revenues, had dropped him as a distributor. It was nothing he did wrong, other than being small; it turns out a larger competitor lost its competing line when the manufacturer took all sales efforts in-house and his vendor switched to the larger competitor. What makes this even sadder is that the same thing happened to him years before; he lost his top line and it devastated his business. Pay attention to the number and health of your vendors as they can disrupt operations almost

You are between your vendors and your customers. While customers are the most important part of any business (along with employees), vendors are not far behind. Earlier I shared a story about a former client who lost two top vendors, years apart. In both cases it put his income and business at risk.

What is your relationship with your vendors? Is it a partnership or are you just a customer they sell to? At some point, before any deal closes, you will have to introduce a buyer to your vendors, if for no other reason than the vendor may want to approve credit. Are you confident enough in your vendor relationships to pick up the phone today, call your vendors, and introduce a buyer (or even discuss sensitive supply issues)? If not, you need to get to the point where you can easily make that call.

How in tune with your vendors' situation are you? (One could easily flip this around and ask if your customers are in tune with your situation.) Do you talk to them about any lines that might be discontinued, their material pricing issues and how it affects you, any product changes they foresee, and any changes to the way they do business?

As you strive to prepare your business for the smoothest exit possible, at the highest price, this is one area where a little effort can make a huge difference in how a buyer perceives your business.

Pragmatic vendor issues

How are your prices set? Are they negotiated or do you buy off a price list? Do quantity discounts make it worthwhile to have high vendor concentration, or should you pay a little more to have multiple suppliers? The right answer for one business may not be the right answer for another.

What about your credit terms? More importantly, what about the credit terms the new owner might get? If you're taking a discount for paying immediately, will the buyer be able to continue that in addition to making acquisition debt payments? These are important issues. The tighter your relationship with your vendors, the better the terms your buyer will receive.

Real-Life Story

Desperation was in the voice on the other end of the phone call. Doug was less than a week from closing on an acquisition when he found out that the seller had no credit with his suppliers; he paid everything COD. Doug's cash flow model assumed he had an average of thirty days to pay his bills.

Was this sloppy due diligence? Of course it was. Doug was my client, so I simply asked him what the seller told him when he asked question thirty-two on the due diligence questionnaire. After hemming and hawing he admitted he hadn't asked it. This is what happens when buyers get buyer fever. They ignore common sense and don't want to ask all the questions they should ask.

> ***As a seller, you want to make sure the buyer has all necessary information. Doug's sloppiness almost derailed his deal. After all the time and effort both sides put into this, not to mention the expense, it would have been devastating to both buyer and seller for the deal to collapse because of this.***

Do you have a choice of vendors with competitive products and prices? This is the ideal situation. However, at all sizes of companies vendor concentration is often a bottleneck, or dependency. Consider the 2011 Japan earthquake and tsunami and what it did to the automobile industry. Not only Japanese firms were affected; Ford had supply problems because of the quantity of parts they bought in Japan.

Boeing had massive issues with their 787 Dreamliner delivery schedule. Many of the problems were because of the work outsourced to subcontractors (a vendor of sorts, providing a completed section or part, not just materials).

Don't let the lease disrupt your deal

Often overlooked until late in the process, the lease can be a critical area. Unless you are a consulting or accounting firm, a bank may not give your buyer a loan for a term any longer than the term of your lease including fixed options. It's expensive to move and the bank (and buyer) doesn't want the business uprooted in the middle of the loan.

A landlord's willingness to assign the lease or give a buyer a new lease at a fair rate is also important. The supply and demand for the type of space your company needs is one of the biggest factors in all of this. If supply is tight, a landlord can play tough. If supply greatly exceeds demand, the landlord will do everything possible to keep the business as a tenant.

Real-Life Story

The shareholder agreement dictated that if one of the equal owners of a food manufacturing business wanted out, the other had to purchase the shares (after a prescribed process). During the valuation process, we discovered that there was no lease, the landlord was elderly and quite ill, and the landlord and his daughter wanted to get rid of all the small tenants in the building and find one or two large tenants.

The cost of a forced move with thirty days' notice was equal to one year's profit. The value of the company declined by over 30 percent. Within six months of the buyout, the owner made an orderly, planned move at a reasonable cost. Financially, he was way ahead. Emotionally, he was even further ahead.

Any smart buyer, whether getting a bank loan or not, will want lease protection.

Real-Life Story

Jerry's company made saw blades, and we were doing a national search for other saw blade manufacturers to acquire. Jerry's plan was to move some or all of the production into his facility, where he had excess capacity.

As part of the planning for this project, we talked about his factory, his lease, and the capacity for growth. The bottom line was this highly profitable company couldn't afford to move. The cost to move massive machinery, the improvements to any new space, and the disruption would devastate the bottom line. Most manufacturing, distribution, and especially retail businesses can't afford to move unless it's because of fast growth; and even then it's still an expensive disruption.

Buying and selling a business is about relationships. The same is true regarding your landlord and your lease. Having a good relationship with your landlord can help your sale, make the buyer comfortable, and get you a higher price and better terms.

The condition of your local commercial real-estate market may dictate what happens in this area. A strong market may make a landlord demand higher rent, a shorter term, and more nebulous renewal options. While analyzing a company for a sale to the company's CEO, I reviewed the lease and its renewal terms. The lease stated that it could be renewed at the "then-fair market rental value." Not much protection to the lease here, is there?

Your facilities are a big part of your company's growth potential. If you are bursting at the seams, what are the buyer's options? If you have twenty thousand square feet and need ten thousand square feet, what does that mean to a buyer who also has to make acquisition debt payments? Can you add a second shift? Does a remote location make sense? What about zoning limitations? All of these will be of concern to a buyer, so have a handle on them.

As I am not a commercial real-estate expert, I've asked Adam Mihlstin with Washington Partners to contribute on this subject in more detail and a lot better than I can.

Transfer Rights and How They Impact the Real Estate Lease in Selling or Buying a Business

"Flexibility has become a modern-day value that everyone wants. But flexibility comes with a cost." —Maynard Webb, technology executive and angel investor

When negotiating the real-estate lease for a new business, it's easy for little or no thought to be given to selling the business (months or years later). However, understanding various exit strategies and negotiating favorable terms at the outset provides significant flexibility and benefits down the road. Flexibility is a benefit with immeasurable value when the transfer of lease rights comes into play.

The best advice for anyone engaging in real-estate matters is to seek counsel from a trusted advisor, a professional with the proper credentials. Consult with experienced professionals—a commercial real-estate broker and/or real-estate lawyer—to protect your interests and illuminate the advantages and pitfalls inherent in any real-estate transaction.

There are two principle ways to transfer your interest in a real-estate lease. Transfer is either completed by assignment or sublease. Although both actions transfer your interest, assignment and sublease clauses have vastly different legal and practical outcomes.

Assign or Sublease–What's the Difference?

An **assignment** is the complete transfer of rights (from the assignor to the assignee) defined in the lease. The assignee becomes the new tenant. The assignee pays rent directly to the landlord and is responsible for all the terms and conditions of the lease. However, caveat emptor...there are varying degrees to which the landlord will release you from the lease obligations.

A **sublease** is a separate agreement between the seller and purchaser. The original landlord becomes the "master landlord," the seller becomes the "sublandlord," and the purchaser becomes the "subtenant." A sublease can be for a portion or all of the leased premises. The sublease references the master lease agreement and generally holds all parties responsible to the terms and conditions originally negotiated. The sublandlord is responsible for rent payments and collects it from the subtenant. The sublandlord shouldn't expect to make a significant profit by capitalizing on a strong real-estate leasing market. Savvy landlords cap the amount the sublandlord can collect and share in the profits.

Liability–Who's Responsible for What?

Transferring your lease rights to another party doesn't always relieve you of your lease obligations. Should the assignee or subtenant default on any of the lease terms and conditions, the landlord could terminate the lease and seek financial compensation from you. Even with an assignment, the landlord might still require you to be an active participant until the lease expires. The obvious benefit to the landlord is that you might be in a financially better position to compensate the landlord should there be a default.

What Are the Key Issues?

When considering the future of your lease rights, the following areas of concern should be thought out carefully to successfully complete your assignment or sublease:

- **Flexibility**—Properly and strategically worded lease language keeps your options open. A good real-estate attorney can provide the proper language to insert into the lease.

- **Reasonable consent from landlord**—To expedite the negotiation process, conduct preliminary discussions with the landlord to predetermine if the landlord will unreasonably condition, deny, or delay approval of the assignment or sublease. You should deal with this step as soon as reasonably possible.

- **Release from liability**—This is the optimal arrangement, if you can secure it from the landlord. As noted above, the landlord will want to have as much (financial) security as possible, and that might mean having both parties fully responsible for the obligations of the lease for the entire lease term. When evaluating the credibility of the assignee or subtenant, the landlord's review will generally include the net worth, property use, and reputation of the incoming party.

- **Right of recapture**—This provision allows the landlord to take back the space should the assignee or subtenant default. Remembering that flexibility is your key advantage, for any number of reasons you might need to take back the purchaser's interest and continue to run the business. To avoid any disturbance in business continuity, it's critical to not lose your interest in the leased premises.

- **Profit from rent**—Specific to a sublease arrangement, it can be fiscally beneficial to retain a portion of the rent that exceeds the original amount owed to the landlord. You'll want to negotiate an equitable split of this revenue with the landlord on any excess rents collected.

- **Plan, plan, and plan ahead**—Easier said than done. However, define the timeline for landlord approval and the other necessary steps to successfully transfer the rights; leave ample time to complete negotiations and documentation.

Conclusion

Every business situation is different with no simple answer or process for determining if subletting or assigning lease rights is the correct choice. Seeking qualified counsel, using sound business policies, and keeping the lines of communication open between all parties are essential to success.

Adam Mihlstin can be reached at 425-894-8153 or amihlstin@earthlink.net.

Access to capital

What does your banker think of your industry? Will the banker demand a buyer have direct industry experience (as with restaurants) or will general business management skills suffice? What about your business in particular? Are your receivables collected fast enough to make the bank happy? Do you have adequate cash flow to meet your debt coverage ratios? And the most important question: Can the business, in its current state, handle acquisition debt?

Real-Life Story
In another example of one partner selling to another, the banker made it very clear that he would do whatever he could to support the buyer. He loved the business; he loved the buyer and his attention to financial details. In practical terms, this support meant that the selling partner could be removed from the loan guarantees, which was something the buying partner did not expect and thought would be a sticking point in getting a deal done.

There is a good chance your buyer will get a bank loan to make the acquisition. This will, most of the time, necessitate the buyer using the acquisition-funding bank for all banking needs. That said, the new banker doesn't have a relationship with the business. He doesn't have the insights your current banker has, and that means he will, at least at first, play things "by the book."

What does that mean to you? It means you should have your business ready for a new bank. Be diligent about the following items:

- Billings
- Accounts receivable and their collections
- Lines of credit (use them and pay them off)
- Inventory management
- Quality and timely financial statements

The Five Cs of banking

When I started in the consulting business, banks were big on the Five Cs, in the rah-rah days of cheap credit (the mid-2000s) they didn't seem to matter, and then, poof, we're back to where we were. The emphasis now is "How do we get paid back?" Keep in mind that the Five Cs go back to before anyone reading this was born.

Whether you are dependent on a bank or not, pay attention to this because the chances are your buyer will need a bank to fund operations and growth, and the more your business is attractive to a bank, the more confident a buyer will be (meaning a better price, better terms, easier process, and perhaps a quicker payoff to you).

Capacity—How will you repay the money? There had better be cash flow to support your debt payments or why would anybody lend you the money? Without capacity, you'll be dependent on the next factor.

Collateral—What does the lender get if you can't make the payments? Believe me, the bank does not want your truck, house, car, equipment, or anything else. The bank wants to be repaid, and thus is it severely discounts the value of the assets used as collateral.

Capital—This is your skin in the game, also known as your risk. As in the story below, your capital (as an owner, buyer, or seller) is more important than it was in recent years.

Conditions—What is the loan for? Banks usually want to tie long-term needs (a piece of equipment or a business acquisition) to a term loan. Short-term needs (working capital) will be tied to a line-of-credit loan, like an accounts receivable line of credit that will be paid back when your customer pays you.

Character—Like you selling your product, or selling your business, it's a relationship game with your banker. You must come across as competent, trustworthy, experienced, and of solid reputation.

Real-Life Story

Mike Flynn, former publisher of the **Puget Sound Business Journal** *and now active in the world of raising capital, spoke at my Rotary Club. When talking about banking, he said the following:*

"The most important change [in banking] is that the days when a business owner could get new capital without putting up a key chunk of himself or herself are over. The point now being made by those with money to place is this: If you aren't confident enough in your business and its prospects to mortgage your house and put your life savings into it, then why should I have confidence in you? Now is the time for maximum skin in the game. As the chairman of a Washington State–based bank told me later, 'That should always have been the case. It wasn't. But it is now. And it will be in the future.'"

My experience is that if it's a good deal (for the borrower and the bank), banks will make the loan. A good deal means adequate debt coverage, a quality borrower, and enough collateral (which can be the cash flow, especially in SBA-guaranteed situations).

For insights into your buyer's SBA lending world, here's an essay from Lisa Forrest, a Small Business Administration (SBA) lending officer with Union Bank in Bellevue, WA.

PUTTING TOGETHER A BUSINESS LOAN PACKAGE

How you prepare your business for sale and how your buyer applies for a loan can help increase your odds for a successful sale with more cash to you!

With all that we've heard about the tight credit market, one important fact seems overlooked: banks are in the business of lending. Would-be sellers can increase the feasibility of a lender wanting to help finance an acquisition loan for a buyer through thoughtful preparation and attention to details. And currently the Small Business Administration (SBA) loan program is an excellent avenue that banks can use for business acquisition financing. The SBA has certain guidelines and parameters that every participating bank must follow when offering this type of loan; however, each lender will have its own requirements and terms, at times causing increased confusion and some amount of trepidation. While the uncertainties of these economic times mixed with inconsistencies in the banking environment can be unsettling for business owners considering a sale, there are definite steps owners can follow to control critical aspects of the sales process when it comes to acquisition financing.

Here are nine points for the seller to consider that can help make the business a stronger candidate for SBA acquisition financing:

1. **Business owner planning and preparation**—Planning to sell your business can take years. Knowing when it is the right time to sell takes thought and preparation. For most of the successful acquisitions I have been involved with, preparation started months, and in most cases several years, prior to the actual loan/acquisition close. Being a prepared and organized seller is key.

2. **Exit strategy advisors**—Because your business is usually one of your biggest investments, having outside advice is generally going to increase your opportunities for success. As an owner, you are an expert in your industry and have built a successful business; however, when it comes to selling your gem that you have spent years creating, I have observed that outside expertise and perspective will usually serve the seller well. See number one above.

3. **Buyers and lenders**—These two groups have similar perspectives. The buyer and lender will have the same

questions and want to see the same documentation, books, and records. The buyer's and banker's interests are well aligned, so when you think about questions that the bank will have, they are most often the same questions that your buyer will have. This is an important notion to understand because a seller should be preparing for the buyer and the banker in much the same way.

4. **Buyer "due diligence team"**—As a banker specializing in business acquisition financing for more than twenty years, I have come to appreciate the buyer who has his or her own due diligence team. And, as a seller, you should come to appreciate this as well. When buyers come with outside advisors, it signals to me that they are serious and prepared to take the process all the way through to a close. This team usually consists of a CPA, attorney, banker, and buyer representative. And, for sellers that are prepared, having a buyer with a team of trusted, experienced acquisition advisors will actually help move the process along faster.

5. **Documentation for a bank loan package**—Having your financial documents organized, up to date, and ready for the buyer's lender is critical. Generally, the lender will *initially* require three years of business tax returns, year-end financial statements, and year-to-date financial statements including profit and loss statement, balance sheet, accounts receivable, payables aging statements, and debt schedule. The lender will also require three years' personal tax returns on the buyer, personal financial statement, and complete resume. The buyer's background, industry experiences, and complementary work history is also critical for consideration. Letter of intent on the transaction will be required for initial underwriting. If initially available, copies of leases are helpful at the outset. These are

the basic documentation requirements to get the package started and additional information will be required along the way depending on each specific project.

6. **Lender underwriting…business considerations**—Once your buyer has submitted a complete loan package, the bank's underwriter will generally take about two to three weeks to thoroughly review the loan request. Each lender will have its own credit policies, but because the business acquisition project is usually lacking full collateralization, lenders will generally require acceptable debt service. Your business's existing cash flow must show the ability to cover the requested bank debt, appropriate salary for the buyer's personal living needs, plus a "cushion" or margin for error on top. The lender will also analyze performance trends. An organized seller will have prepared, in advance, explanations for any unusual adjustments, seller discretionary add-backs, or negative performance issues. Having written statements ready for the buyer's lender always impresses. Having access to the seller's CPA can also be a help to the lender during underwriting, especially if there are interesting adjustments or complicated add-backs to more clearly understand.

7. **Lender underwriting and buyer qualifications**—The lender is going to look for the following in your buyer: industry and/or complementary work expertise, resources available for down payment and postclosing personal liquidity, collateral support, credit score, and secondary sources of repayment.

8. **Mitigations**—In a perfect world, the lender would review a project with 100 percent positive trends in all areas of debt service, performance trends, buyer industry experience, and liquidity. In all my years of SBA lending, it has been a rare occurrence to

have a project with perfect scores in all areas. That's what makes my job fun. There is a real art to helping put an SBA acquisition project together. As lenders, we are always trying to find the right blend of loan amount, buyer down payment, and seller carry-back financing to balance the particular strengths and challenges of each specific acquisition project. The more prepared the seller is for the buyer's underwriting process, the more the seller can play a positive role in providing critical information and being sensitive to what the buyer is experiencing.

9. **Be open to the financing process**—Take a deep breath and persevere. I don't mean to sound too dramatic, but lenders are going to get nosy. Please understand that the lender asks all these questions and requires the documentation simply to learn about the merit of your specific project. I never seek to offend but only to understand. I have the utmost respect for business owners who have spent years building something of value, and my goal is to reach a win-win-win for the seller, buyer, and bank. I love my job because I always…always… come away from each project knowing more than I did when I started. And I find, with the right mind-set and preparation, the same can be said for all involved.

Lisa Forrest can be reached at 425-999-2042 or lisaforrest@comcast.net.

Advisors

It's important that you have an advisory team. Make sure your attorney is experienced in buy-sell deals. The same goes for your CPA (some don't know transaction tax, they just do tax returns). You may also use an intermediary to help market the company. There aren't too many more advisors you'll need; it's the buyer who may have HR people, environmental consultants, or others to assist in specific areas.

Technology

Let's step back and be sure you can answer the question "How does your business benefit from the technology in which you've invested?" Today, all businesses use technology (or should).

The buyer will be interested in the answers. If you are not using technology effectively, it may be an opportunity a buyer sees and acts upon. Of course, you might not get paid as high a price as if you can demonstrate how efficient you are.

There are three areas that you need to keep current: hardware, software, and the Internet.

Hardware is the most obvious. One company had a mix of old computers and an antiquated server (in 2010). Some were on Windows XP, some on Windows 98, and one was still on Windows 95. The buyer saw this as a capital investment and this factor was used in his negotiations. The small investment in hardware is well worth it.

Software is often in the background and it can be your place to shine. Make sure you know what you use and that it's all up to date and legal. If you have proprietary software, a buyer may want to know the costs to keep it current and increase its productivity factor. Be able to explain why you chose the particular software.

A website is a necessity for almost all businesses these days. Yes, there are a few that don't need or want one, but they are the exception. Buyers will want to know who does your hosting, who maintains your website, what it costs, what domain names you have registered, where they are registered, and when any registrations expire. Security issues are at the top of the list on technology due diligence, especially if you deal with secure information. Be able to explain your security protocols, protection software and firewalls, offsite access, and anything else that could be an issue (to your business and to a buyer).

The bottom line is, if you can show a buyer that your systems are up to date, adequate for growth, and your people know how to be productive on them, it's one item you can cross off the due diligence list.

Marketing

After the word *potential* the next most common word used by business sellers is *marketing*. It's used in and with the context of "If a buyer knows anything about marketing, there is so much potential in this business." Of course, the implication is that the buyer with marketing experience should pay for all that potential (before it's realized).

What a buyer hears is "They've tried every marketing technique known and sales are still where they are. How am I going to do better?"

One could spend a lifetime reading about marketing and how to do it better. As a business owner, you need to be able to answer the following three questions that a buyer will (or should) ask:

1. What is your marketing strategy and its tactics?

2. Do you have an actual plan for point one; do you document what you do and track results?

3. Do you have cost-benefit metrics (i.e., what are the actual results from your marketing efforts)?

Marketing can be one important part of your competitive advantage. In the mid-nineties, when I was active with my local Chamber of Commerce, I realized that when the Chamber did events, there were two topics that put people in the seats: money and marketing, and I doubt if things have changed.

Real-Life Example

A simple breakeven analysis can be applied to marketing. Let's assume your contribution margin (sales less all variable costs) is 40 percent. Divide a new expense, a marketing campaign, for example, by 40 percent to find the amount of new sales you need to make the campaign run at breakeven.

If you spend $10,000 on marketing, you need $25,000 of new additional sales to reach breakeven on the campaign (10,000/.40). If sales increase by $100,000 you have $40,000 of additional contribution margin and the marketing program gave you a four-to-one return.

Of course, in real life, it's not usually this easy. Marketing efforts, other than direct-response–type coupons, aren't instantaneous, require repetition, and may just be part of an overall sales strategy with other variables.

More important is to show what happened before you started any marketing campaign or what happens if you stop it. Most important is to show you have a handle on your marketing.

Competition

"The company doesn't have any competition" will never impress a savvy buyer. Every business has competition, and if it doesn't you (and your buyer) should be worried. You don't want to be perceived as similar to the floppy-disk industry in the early 2000s. Sure, there wasn't much competition, but that was when Apple, followed by PC manufacturers, stopped putting floppy drives in computers.

A buyer will research your competition, as it's easier to do these days than ever before. I've seen situations where buyers have known more about the competition than the owner.

This is where the term "competitive advantage" comes to the forefront. Be able to coherently explain what your advantage is over your competitors and what advantages they may have over you.

I have written numerous articles for and spoken at the national convention of the Non Ferrous Foundry Society whose members are foundries that do materials other than steel (brass, gold, bronze, etc.). In researching the industry for my speech, I found out that these small

US-based foundries have an advantage over China when it comes to prototypes, small runs, immediate needs, and custom products. Chinese foundries have an advantage in large orders with long lead times.

The foundry industry has huge barriers to entry. Not every business or industry is so fortunate. It's incredibly easy to start a staffing agency, a janitorial business, or a restaurant. However, in these industries, where there are constant start-ups and franchising (often the indication an industry has low barriers to entry) there are also large, dominant players. As with foundries, there are advantages to many different types of companies.

Real-Life Story

When my children were active in youth sports, there were two or three large sporting goods firms in the Seattle area that provided uniforms and equipment. A start-up uniform company in our area started in the owner's garage for production and his basement for the office.

The competitive advantages were initially price and service. The price part was easy because the company had almost no overhead. The service took time. I recall the owner went to many, many Little League and soccer association board meetings to build relationships and demonstrate that his quality was the same as the big stores'.

Fast forward a few years and this company now has a location in an industrial park (still no expensive retail space). His prices had to increase, but the company still maintained the relationships and kept its customers.

What are the barriers to entry in your industry? They could be capital requirements, licensing requirements (a specific certification for someone on the staff or FDA approval, for example), knowledge, geographic location, or something else. No matter what they are, be able to articulate them.

You should know the following:

- Is there a threat from a large competitor? Or are you the large competitor in your industry able to muscle smaller firms?
- Do you or your competitors have a product or engineering advantage?
- Who has any production advantages?
- Are there any shipping advantages?
- Are there service and quality differences that are reflected in the price?

To summarize, know your competition—is it friendly or cutthroat and how difficult is it to enter the industry? This is what you should know and a buyer will definitely want to know.

A company doing $5 million in sales had a handful of competitors, including one that was about fifteen times larger. One of the competitor's employees accepted a job with the smaller firm and the larger firm sued him. His new employer got caught in the middle and it cost the company over $60,000.

One of the risks identified was the threat of another lawsuit from this large competitor. The competitor had a much greater capacity for legal bills, and as the smaller company gained market share there were constant hints of more lawsuits. This is the kind of thing that will scare many buyers, so it pays to be knowledgeable.

Chapter Seven

They're not buying your business–they're buying your people

"I'm interested in your employees because while technically I'm buying the business, what I'm really buying are the people that make the business what it is." A buyer said this to a seller, a seller who didn't understand why the buyer needed to talk to his key employees before closing the deal.

Your people are your business; not much more can be said about their importance to any company. You may have invented a fantastic product, but someone has to make that product. Have the best service in town? It's because your people provide that service. Is your customer base wider and deeper than your competitors'? Most likely it's because your sales staff is great at generating new customers and maintaining solid customer relationships.

For the purpose of making your business as attractive as possible to a buyer, let's focus on three areas. These areas, and their subsets, are the areas I have found buyers are the most interested in knowing about. Put time into preparing your employee structure, culture, and systems, and buyers will be impressed. Focus on the following areas:

1. The pragmatic, including what your employees do, what they're paid, what are their metrics and how they can advance within the company.

2. The softer side, including teamwork, your culture, delegation, and similar

3. Compliance with rules, regulations, and benefits

I am not anywhere close to an expert on human resources and its policies and requirements, so at the end of this chapter there is an essay by one of my guest contributors, Jack Goldberg, that covers HR rules and guidelines.

Employees should be employees

Initial questions will center on the quality of the management team and key employees. As with customers, the more spread out the responsibilities of employees, the better for the business (and you).

It can be tough for an entrepreneur, but you have to learn to delegate if you're not doing it now. Contrary to what many company founders and owners believe, it is not a sign of losing control. In fact, delegating responsibility is the opposite—it's gaining control.

Real-Life Story

Owners often have a mental block against delegating because they feel the employees don't have the same passion for the business. (They don't and won't when getting paid $15 to $20 per hour). Therefore, the owner's feelings are, "I can do anything better than anybody else, so I'll be involved in every aspect of the business."

Sam had this attitude. It didn't matter that on accounting and finance he was a novice, he gave instructions to his accounting department. He could sell his product like nobody else, so any closing ratio less than his meant an incompetent salesperson. Thinking on the job was a waste of time; employees needed to be constantly "doing." Anyone found not being busy was admonished.

It was no wonder he constantly worried about everything, even when things were going well. It took a while to get him to allow his people to use their skills and to coach them, not admonish them. But it worked, and he had a much stronger team.

Before we discuss the above topics, make sure that you are not breaking the law by treating people who should be employees as independent contractors. I know that the vast majority of people reading this are doing the right thing. However, while writing this book, I've experienced two instances of companies either violating the statutes or operating in a very gray area. If in doubt, get a professional opinion. Your buyer probably will.

A winning culture

Determining the culture in a small business is not that easy from the outside. Given that buyers are by nature skeptical, they will assume the culture is mediocre at best until you show them it's better. Here are three areas I have found buyers will want to know about and be able to investigate: chemistry, delegation, and structure. As I am not a teamwork and culture specialist, following my explanation of these three subjects is an essay from Libby Wagner, who helps companies create a culture of profit.

Chemistry—If you watch sports at all, you inevitably hear commentators talk about team chemistry. Often the most talented team doesn't win the championship, or even the game, because the less talented team plays better together. In other words, they maximize the benefit of teamwork. You have to lead the effort to create teamwork.

There are team-building activities like participating in a charity event as a team, rock climbing, or zip-lining together. But cohesion has to sustain longer than a few hours or a couple days. One client's company has an annual Christmas party where one of the bosses plays Monty Hall and they do a version of "Let's Make a Deal." The employees all win, and they love not only the gifts but also the atmosphere. Libby will write more on this; my point is that a buyer can sniff out problems in this area.

Real-Life Story

Mark suspected it; to him it spelled opportunity, and after closing on his acquisition he confirmed it by giving the management team a short survey. To a person, they all answered the question "What is the company's biggest weakness?" with a version of this (actual) answer, "The biggest weakness just walked out the door."

Employees will be nice when meeting a buyer, but at the same time, it's tough to disguise culture problems. Mark had sensed that the seller, an industry veteran who had worked his way up from the shop floor to owning a business had a "my way or the highway" attitude that was stifling the company. He was right, the management team was extremely capable and welcomed the chance to contribute (similar to my mention in chapter two of the employee who said, "He's been a breath of fresh air").

Don't do what your employees can do

Delegate—I've used the word dependency quite a few times in previous chapters. It is absolutely critical that you eliminate the most critical dependency a firm can have and that is when everything, or a majority of things, are dependent on the owner's involvement. I've seen companies with over fifty employees where the owner was the key cog in the operations and I remember one company with twelve employees where we determined it was really an eleven-person operation because the owner did almost nothing.

Delegating is not always easy, especially to a founder who knows the product or operations as well as anybody in the industry. It does take letting go. Before that it takes hiring the right people. Believe me, a buyer would prefer to hear that you have great employees with a salary range at the high end than that you have mediocre employees at the low end of the salary range.

I was taught that delegating has three components:

1. You (and your management team) must be willing to delegate. This is often the toughest element. It can be hard to let go, to let people stumble and bruise themselves (and hurt the company a little). But if you don't let them stumble and learn on small things, what happens when they are forced to deal with big issues?

2. Your employees at all levels must be willing to accept delegation. Some people just don't want responsibility and they are easy to sort out. It's the people who do want to grow, advance, and contribute that you want to nurture and train. They will rise to the top, volunteer to take on projects, and be willing to learn.

3. There must be a culture where delegation is acceptable. Pick up any business publication and chances are you will find an article on the workplace, bad managers, good managers, or similar. You may be willing to delegate, employees may be willing to accept delegation, and others, usually not as capable, will not accept it and may actually sabotage it. Perhaps they are jealous they weren't delegated to or promoted. In any event,

if you can make delegation acceptable, it will impress your buyers (who all want to grow and use your team to do so).

Real-Life Story

Behind his back, employees referred to Steve's "drive-bys." He had a habit of hovering over an employee's desk or cubicle, fidgeting for a minute or two, then blurting out something like, "Don't worry about that, it's just my money" and stomping off. Nice culture of appreciation, isn't it?

Tom did things differently. He was a sales guy and knew he had to let his management team handle the operations, production, and administration in his eighty-people-plus company. His six-person management team worked well together, they knew their roles, and their employees loved them. I know firsthand because after I worked with this firm I had them do some work for me. What a difference when the employees at all levels are empowered and respected.

People Due Diligence: How do you know if a company has the right culture for profitable success?

The following essay on company culture is from Libby Wagner. Sometimes, business buyers make the mistake of looking only at the P&L or balance sheet when making a decision to buy a business. Certainly, looking at the financial picture, the business history, and the potential market are all important in the process of making the best decision for you. What buyers often overlook, however, is whether or not the organization can sustain a big change like a buy-out or owner transfer to keep things moving along toward profitability and growth, two characteristics that most want for business performance.

Organizational culture exists, and the question all business leaders should consider is whether this culture is *accidental* or *intentional.* Sometimes, especially with small to medium-sized businesses, leaders or owners have created initial success with an entrepreneurial spirit and they haven't really taken time to articulate the important elements that they desire in their company culture. Or, they haven't created the systems and processes to support that positive, profit-building culture. If you are selling a business, realize your buyer may want to make changes and create new ways of doing things, but make no mistake, there is a culture currently operating in this business, and you will need to determine whether or not it is resilient enough to stay on track through the changes that will naturally occur with a business buy-out.

Here are three areas to examine and some questions to expect from a buyer:

1. What is the relationship like between the employees and the managers? Especially ask about the following:
   a. What's the level of trust—low, medium, or high?
   b. How do employees receive feedback about work performance?
   c. Can the employees clearly articulate the business mission and vision?
   d. What happens when things go wrong?

2. Look for indicators of "organizational drag," or those silent costs that erode profit margins and the bottom line. These may include:
   a. Lowered performance
   b. Interpersonal strife and conflict
   c. Unresolved "history" or issues
   d. Increased costs
   e. Turnover in employees
   f. Absenteeism or misuse of leave time (medical/personal)
   g. Frequent miscommunication

h. Lower team function
i. Missed goals and deadlines
j. Missed opportunities for innovation and creativity

3. How are people recognized and rewarded for the following:
    a. Consistent performance?
    b. Above-and-beyond performance?
    c. Long-term performance?

4. What is the current communication infrastructure?
    a. Do supervisors and employees meet regularly for one-on-ones to discuss performance (not resolve day-to-day issues, but specifically for performance)?
    b. Do the leaders have regular, systematic ways of updating the company, interacting with the workers, and getting to know them?
    c. What systems are in place for encouraging transparency, i.e., "speaking the truth to the top"?
    d. How transparent are the decision-making processes?

Shifting in ownership or leadership is a significant change for any company and successful ones make sure that they manage the cultural elements in that change. In general, you cannot communicate too much, and preparing the items above will give you some indication of where you might want to focus your efforts to make sure you are supporting the best culture for profitable success!

Libby Wagner is president of Libby Wagner & Associates and Influencing Options. Her book, The Influencing Option: The Art of Building a Profit Culture in Business *helps leaders develop practical, immediately useable skills for leading high-performing teams in the best environments to support high profits.* Libby can be reached at www.libbywagner.com or 206-906-9203.

Structure

Earlier I provided a small sample org chart. The important question is what does it mean to a buyer? Most buyers will want to know there is a chain of command. It doesn't work when three managers can each give staff members instructions or assign tasks, as in the earlier Real-Life Story. This causes conflicting instructions or deadlines.

This is also important because buyers are interested in growth and growth is easier achieved if there is a proper structure and systems for getting work done. Some of the best buyers I've seen, whether I've been on the buy side or sell side, are those most interested in the company's people and their abilities.

Pragmatic stuff

There is a three-legged stool regarding employees and whether they stay post-transaction. Everybody wants the employees to stay, and everybody is fearful they will leave or be asked to leave.

The following points show that all parties want the employees to stay in their jobs:

- The seller wants loyal people to keep their (good) jobs and have security.

- The buyer is buying the people and is afraid the employees will leave and disrupt the business.

- The employees are fearful of the buyer bringing in her own people.

Everybody wants the same result, that the employees stay, which makes sense because the people are the lifeblood of the business. So, let's look at what a buyer will be interested in (and what you will be interested in if you are thinking of growing by acquisition before exiting).

Getting employee feedback before the buyer does

The larger your business, the more a buyer will be interested in, and the more evidence there will be of chemistry, structure, and delegation. No matter what the size of your business, all buyers will be interested in, or should be interested in, what is in this section.

When discussing customers, I asked you to consider a customer satisfaction survey. Apply the same type of questioning to your employees (better yet, have an outsider interview them). Ask yourself, what is my relationship with my employees? More importantly, how would your employees describe their relationship with you and the company in general?

I've been involved in many employee interviews, both in individual and group settings. It's amazing how smart the employees usually are. Above I gave the example of Mark and how the owner he acquired the business from didn't respect his managers' opinions or ideas.

Unfortunately, that is all too common and usually stems from poor management skills (not knowing what to do) and not from being a control freak or dictator.

Your employees see things from a different perspective than you do, and that can be valuable. Below are some comments and ideas generated from companies where I did one-on-one employee feedback interviews or facilitated group sessions. All were done without the owner present if it was the management team in the session and without both the owner and the management team present if it was only the employees in the session. Here is some of what they said:

- The owner is too nice; he can't say no to the customers and it spreads the company too thin.
- We don't get enough money upfront from customers and it causes cash-flow issues.
- We wasted a lot of money, and better communication would help.
- The company needs more key people and more supervision.
- This is a good place to work; we like the owners and hope they succeed and we can stay here.
- Define the role of the number-two person; he is too scattered and doesn't have time to provide direction.
- Eliminate redundancies between departments.
- Establish stricter customer expectations.
- Increase lead times to reduce rework.

- Have more focused meetings and increase standardization of processes.

- We "panic manage" too much.

- Increased and improved cross-training will improve operations and reduce bottlenecks.

- Improve communication between departments.

- We don't know what the expectations are.

- There is a lack of teamwork, part of which is caused by a lack of briefings.

- Our field people need more training.

Real-Life Story

I promise complete anonymity when doing interviews. In other words, I will share with my client a summary of all comments and ideas but will not identify the employee if it is a criticism. I must appear to be very trustworthy (which I believe I am) because employees really open up to me.

The trust factor is extremely important. During one group session, the wife of the owner walked in about halfway through the meeting. She worked in the accounting department, so technically she was an employee. Boy, did the atmosphere cool and fast. The employees saw her as a spy, not a coemployee who wanted to contribute, and their comments went from blunt to sanitized, reducing the effectiveness of the session.

One part of the exercise I've found critical is to ask the owner and management team what they think the employees will say is important to improve the company. Remember, when a buyer interviews your people, you won't be there. By doing this in advance, you will uncover areas you can improve before a buyer comes on the scene.

Real-Life Story

An associate and I met with the management team of a manufacturing company, and they identified eight areas they thought the employees would mention as needing attention. The managers ranked three as critical issues, three as needing work but not critical, and two as "OK," meaning they might need some tweaking at the most.

The employees brought up thirteen issues: they ranked eight as critical, three as not critical, and two as "OK." The management team's issues were predominantly operations focused. Their list included more training on their job-estimating system, more product training, and better scheduling. Overall, the management team hit on less than 50 percent of the issues brought up by employees.

One of the areas management ranked OK was communication. Of the employees' eight critical issues, five were related to communication, with communication between departments on jobs given "super-critical" status.

Things look different from the top. This management team not only missed the bull's-eye, they were barely on the target. Can you imagine a buyer finding out about this dysfunction during due diligence? Some would run, some would negotiate the price down, and others, if they have team-building skills, might see it as an opportunity.

Your employees

One of the first things a buyer will want to see is a list of employees, their total compensation, date of hire, and title. How are compensation levels determined? Are you high, low, or average for your industry and location? You will be asked these questions, so be prepared.

The biggest reason for getting the information should be for the buyer to know how to plan for growth and the cost of people in positions that will need to be expanded.

Here are three things to be careful with as you prepare to sell:

1. Don't give any indication there will be raises for all employees, whether from you or the buyer. One seller actually told the employees the buyer would be giving everybody a raise postclose. It sure shocked the buyer.

2. If you give annual bonuses, and they've become routine and expected, don't tell a buyer they're discretionary. The last thing a buyer wants to do is cancel bonuses because the price was based on pre-bonus income levels.

3. Don't hold back on raises, hiring, or firing because you might sell. Operate the business until closing as if no sale will occur.

Be able to describe, in detail, the availability of competent employees, especially at the management and key-employee level. Also, it's important that you can share how you find people. It could range from Craigslist to retained searches and everything in-between. The higher your turnover rate, the greater the interest in where you find people. Here are three wide and varied examples:

1. The majority of this manufacturing business's employees are machinists. As I write this, there is a tight market for good machinists and the future is predicted to be even tighter. The average machinist age is about fifty-five and the owner is concerned that when this group starts retiring, replacements

will be hard to find, especially in Seattle, where Boeing can skew the labor market.

2. A testing laboratory hires scientists to run the tests. One might think the market for science majors would be tight, but it isn't. There aren't a lot of science jobs if you don't have a PhD, and there is always an availability of technical people.

3. A friend owns a specialty pizza restaurant. While there's turnover of college students for the serving jobs, he's got great longevity in the kitchen. It's a good place to work for a cook (this is not a menu-driven restaurant that needs a chef), he pays a fair wage, and there's a feeling of being part of a team.

Do you have employment agreements and noncompete agreements? Has your attorney recommended you have them, at least for management and salespeople? Don't leave a buyer in no-man's-land on this. Realize that, in most states, a noncompete agreement can't prevent people from earning a living in their field. It usually can prevent an ex-employee from contacting your customers or employees (to recruit them away). As with anything that has legal or tax ramifications, consult your attorney and CPA. Get this area under control as part of your preparation. The more in advance of a sale you do this, the better.

Real-Life Story

We were two weeks away from closing when the deal almost collapsed. My client, the seller, was the owner of a small business. The buyer was a middle-market company that was buying service providers in its niches.

The buyer's president came in one day and said that all employees—yes, all employees, including laborers and clerical staff, would have to sign the standard employment and

noncompete agreement. And if any employee didn't sign the agreement and left employment, the deal would be reevaluated and in jeopardy. To make it more interesting, the agreement was very onerous—the seller's attorney said it was mostly unenforceable.

This deal was crucial to the seller. There weren't any financial buyers for this breakeven business and health issues necessitated a deal sooner than later. One employee held out and wouldn't sign. After talking to the seller's attorney and getting a small bonus (call it a signing bonus, although it was from the seller), she signed and the deal closed.

What does everybody do?

A question I ask every buyer is "What do you want to do on a daily, weekly, and monthly basis?"

A question I ask every seller is "What do you do on a daily, weekly, and monthly basis?"

I've asked hundreds of business buyers this question, and at least 80 percent answer that they want to be involved with strategy, vision, and planning. In addition, they mention areas based on their experience, whether it is marketing, finance and budgeting, or sales. The 20 percent that don't use these words describe their day or week in terms of doing things that involve working "on" the business versus "in" the business (working in the business means doing the day-to-day work necessary to deliver the product to the customer).

If you spend most of your time being CEO and dealing with strategic issues, you are a more attractive acquisition candidate than if you are involved in the day-to-day operations. Financial buyers can easily see themselves in a big-picture role and strategic buyers want a management team.

Equally important is to be able to go beyond job descriptions and discuss what your management team and employees do on a daily, weekly, and monthly basis. Giving examples or telling stories about what they do is more memorable than reading job descriptions. How your team supports you is extremely important because as buyers plan for growth they will rely on the team as much or more than you do.

Employee interviews

In all the deals I've been involved in, I can only think of a handful that were unsuccessful, meaning the buyer struggled or failed. One was a company in the very fickle entertainment industry (and the buyer knew the risks and was willing to roll the dice), a couple losses were for health reasons, but two failures in particular rise to the top of the list: in both cases the seller would not let the buyer talk to the employees or customers before closing.

While this is a small sample size, it is interesting and shows how "buyer fever" can persuade a buyer to bypass a crucial element of due diligence. Of course, given that most sellers will hold a note for part of the price, it is not in the best interest of a seller to hide things from the buyer. Now, some sellers will be glad to get whatever cash they can if they truly believe the employees (or customers) will hurt, if not kill, their deal.

Let's look at a quick list for employee interviews.

Who—Your management team and key employees. This doesn't have to extend to all employees, although I've seen situations where all the employees were brought together for a group meeting before closing to meet the buyer, share ideas, and be assured their jobs were safe. Word travels fast. Once management meets the buyer, the rest of your staff will know what's going on.

What—What will the buyer ask them? Anything and everything may come up, and the only restrictions your employees should have regarding their answers is to not give away any trade secrets. Buyers will mostly be interested in conveying their goals and finding out where the employees see opportunity.

Where—A private room is a must; off-site is best if you don't want the rest of the staff to know what's going on until the interviews are done.

When—This is the *most important* part of employee interviews. Employee interviews happen only after the buyer has completed and checked off everything else on the due diligence list, and often these interviews don't occur until after signing a purchase and sale agreement with a contingency for this and other sensitive matters. This means the buyer has approved due diligence on your financial statements and customers, has a new lease, and everything else is a go. An exception is if you've been very open and all your employees know you are selling. In that case, these interviews come near the end, but you may not wait until all other due diligence items are satisfactorily completed.

Keep in mind that this is also the place where your employees will want to shine for their future boss.

HR: Boring but critically important

Let's finish this chapter with some insights on being compliant with employees. This is a guest article from Jack Goldberg, the CEO of Personnel Management Systems in Kirkland, WA His firm is one of the best human resource outsource firms in the Seattle area. This is an area in which I am not an expert and it is very, very important. There are too many rules, regulations, and laws that can trip up any business if they are not followed correctly. Pay attention to what Jack writes in the following paragraphs and hope that your seller is paying attention to his HR issues.

Don't let them buy an HR problem

Business owners can spend considerable time and resources getting their business ready to sell but somehow fail to address this important area. This is ironic when you consider that for many businesses, payroll and employee benefits can be the first or second largest expense.

This chapter is intended to get you to think about how to get this area of your business in shape—in shape and ready to sell.

Compliance

HR people often think about HR in two ways—*compliance* and *best practices*. Sometimes compliance is seen as "tactical HR" and best practices are seen as "strategic." These labels don't always hold up under every condition, but they can be useful as we attempt to organize a rather diverse, and in some ways complex, part of running a company.

Regardless of whether you are a buyer or seller, taking the time to think through the HR aspects of an organization can pay enormous dividends. At a minimum, it can help eliminate possible deal-breakers.

Compliance issues cover a whole host of topics. This list is intended to be somewhat generic, meaning there could be specific state or local issues that are not listed. And of course, there are most likely industry-specific issues that will need to be addressed.

Documentation

Required documentation for every employee includes current W-4 and I-9 forms. Each I-9 form must be completed correctly or you face thousands of dollars in possible fines if there is an audit. In some industries, audits occur quite frequently. I-9 forms that are not available—or completed incorrectly—raise a red flag of the possibility of illegal workers. Recently, in the process of selling his dry-cleaning business, a friend of mine discovered that several of his key employees were working illegally. Learning this at the point of sale created a huge obstacle for the buyer. I doubt anyone wants to purchase a company only to then have the employees hauled off and deported. Avoid all this by making sure you have legal employees and all the necessary documentation is in place for each employee.

Unemployment Insurance

Virtually all companies pay for and provide unemployment insurance for their employees. Buyers will want to verify that this is in fact the case and that coverage is in place for employees in each state that the company has employees. Second, they'll want to find out what the rate is. Rates are normally experience based, meaning a relatively high rate could indicate frequent layoffs and high employee turnover. A low relative rate would suggest a stable workforce, low turnover, and high retention.

Workers' Compensation

Like unemployment insurance, the rate or premium that a company pays for workers' comp has a lot to do with its experience. A company with a high relative rate may be suggestive of frequent employee accidents or an unsafe work environment. Make sure that coverage is in place for each state and have handy a copy of a claims experience report.

Employment Posters

It may sound silly, but states and the feds require that employers post certain notices. You should have anywhere between eight and ten posters, which are mandated to be conspicuously displayed in a common area (e.g., lunchroom).

EEO-1 Report and/or Affirmative Action Plan

Companies with over a hundred employees are required to complete an annual EEO-1 report. Companies with over fifty employees and government contracts (or subcontractors to government contractors) are required to complete an Affirmative Action Plan (AAP) every year. Not having an AAP means the company is out of compliance with the requirements of the contract. The penalty can be severe and includes cancellation of the government contract(s). AAP preparation is a huge task. If you have one, show it. It should be several inches thick and weigh more than a couple of pounds!

Benefit Plan and Retirement Plan Administration

It is beyond the scope of this essay to talk about all the requirements associated with administering a company's employee benefit plans.

Competent advisors should be engaged to review all employee benefit plans for compliance. However, at the preliminary due diligence stage, some basic questions will be asked. For example, benefit eligibility (which employees get the coverage) should be clear, nondiscriminatory, and consistent with the carrier's contract. It is a red flag if eligibility appears to be arbitrary or discriminatory.

If the company has over twenty employees, it is COBRA eligible. The company should be able to demonstrate competent administration of this program. If not, the company could be exposing itself to huge liability. Part of the COBRA review should also include an audit of the procedure for adding and removing employees from the company benefit plans. More often than not we see sloppy administration in this area. Oftentimes, terminated employees are left on a plan and new employees are not added in a timely fashion.

An organization should also be able to generate plan descriptions and summary plan descriptions (SPD) for each health and welfare type plan.

Minor Work Permits

Many states require work permits for employees under the age of eighteen. There are very clear rules regarding what hours minors can work and what jobs they are allowed to perform. As with many other employment-related regulations, the penalties for noncompliance can be severe.

Wage and Hour Laws

Some people spend their entire professional careers just dealing with wage and hour laws. The area is complex and often counterintuitive. If there is one area of employment regulation that is going to be messed up, it will be this. At a minimum, a buyer should ask some basic questions and, depending on the response, proceed accordingly. For example, ask, "How is overtime being tracked?" The buyer will be very afraid if the response is "Everyone here is salaried" or "We don't pay overtime." Both of these responses indicate a poor understanding of the wage and hour laws and are almost a guarantee that employees are being paid incorrectly. Also, be very leery of a company that can't explain how overtime is calculated, how work time is recorded, or if employees take regular rest and lunch breaks. If administrative employees are working from home or the word "comp time" comes up in your conversation, pay attention. These buzz words are indicative of potential problems that you don't want to inherit.

Harassment Training

Most savvy business owners understand the negative consequences associated with sexual harassment claims. And for good reason, the subject is not something to be taken lightly. I would walk away from any company where I witnessed a callous or disrespectful attitude toward women or minorities or a workplace where bullying is an accepted part of the work culture. Many states require annual harassment training.

Safety

Workplace safety is a necessary part of every work environment. Certainly some industries involve work that is more dangerous than others and will be subject to specific industry requirements on which you should be well versed. Regardless, every company should be able to demonstrate how they have created a safe place to work. Depending on the situation, this may mean having a formal accident prevention program, material safety data sheets (MSDS), CPR training, personal protective equipment, safety committees, and so on. You should be able to review an OSHA log (or equivalent) and notes from a safety committee meeting.

Employee versus Independent Contractor

It should come as no surprise that the states and the federal government dislike when employers classify workers as independent contractors (1099ers) instead of employees. There are many checklists and worksheets available to help a company make a correct determination. A huge red flag should go up if it looks like the determination is made in an arbitrary or nonobjective fashion. If the decision to make an employee an independent contractor was done because it was "less expensive," "easier," or "the employee wanted it that way," it is most surely being done incorrectly!

Best Practices

Along with compliance and tactical issues, HR people also care a lot about what we call HR best practices. In other words, things that aren't necessarily required by a law or regulation but are still good ideas. Perhaps they reduce a company's liability or just make the company a better, more successful organization. Whether or not you are a buyer or seller, you should care about HR best practices. Good HR practices simply result in an overall better company. A company with poor HR practices is asking for trouble and certainly is not operating at its full potential.

Many topics fall into the HR best practices area. The list below is not exhaustive but should give you a feel for what is involved.

Job Descriptions

There is no law that says a company must have job descriptions, but most HR people view them as mission critical. Job descriptions are very useful tools when it comes to hiring, training, compensation, and performance reviews. Without job descriptions, how does one know what the critical skills and experience are of a particular job? How do we know if an applicant is qualified? What is included in a training program? How do we figure out the market rate for compensation? And what are the criteria by which we evaluate the employee's performance? All things that a well-written job description can help us address.

Written Hiring Procedures

Hiring high-quality employees is important for virtually every organization. Before buying a company, I would want to know that some organized effort was being made to hire good people. Evidence of this, at least in part, would be a process that was written down and used. And it is always a good idea to review employee turnover data.

Management Training

Along with quality and competent employees, we want to see competent management. Is there any management training going on? Is the current management team comprised of just high-performing employees who were promoted? How are management skills maintained and developed? Is there any depth on the bench to draw from?

Employee Handbook

Employee polices need to be written down. Lack of written policies is clear evidence of a poorly run "shoot from the hip" company. Clearly articulated polices that are fairly administered are evidence of a professionally run company.

Well-written employee handbooks also substantially help a company follow the applicable employment regulations. This includes everything from administration of leave policies, insurance eligibility, vacation accruals, time keeping, attendance, harassment, and more.

Personnel Files

Before purchasing a company I would always look at the personnel files. Are there copies of performance reviews, disciplinary notices, employment applications, resumes, and so on? You can learn a lot about individual employees as well as the company's organizational skills by reviewing a few key employee files.

Performance Reviews

Certainly not every company does regular performance reviews. However, they can be evidence of a strategic workforce. In other words, performance reviews can be used as a tool to help individuals within an organization move forward and achieve strategic goals. If an organization claims to have strategic goals, I would ask how individuals are measured consistent with these goals. Strategic goals without an employee component could be quite hollow and simply fancy words.

Benefit Plan Design and Cost

It goes without saying that employee benefit plans are costly. However, these costs can be managed. Questions here should involve items such as, How has the plan been designed? What cost-sharing is taking place? Is the plan competitive within the industry? Who is the broker and what services are provided? Strategic thinking means the benefit plan is a component of the overall employee compensation, and some real thought has been put into the "whys" and "hows."

Compensation–What People Are Paid

Too often we find that companies have no rhyme or reason as to how employees are paid. It almost seems random. A well-run company should be able to demonstrate that there is some structure, some rationale, to pay levels. There should be some attempt to ensure both internal equity (employees are being paid fairly compared to one another) and external equity (employees are being paid fairly compared to the outside labor market).

Employee Complaints

Hopefully the employee handbook contains a section on how employee complaints are resolved. If nothing like this exists, then chances are employee problems are being resolved by government agencies (e.g., EEOC) or attorneys. Needless to say, this is not very strategic and demonstrates a lack of professional management or possibly even ambivalence. Buyers should ask about recent employee issues and how they were resolved.

Termination

As with hiring, HR people want to see some written policies around terminations. Are people just "fired" or is there a "progressive disciplinary" approach? Terminations without good documentation oftentimes result in employment-related lawsuits. At a minimum they demonstrate poor management skills.

Reviewing several recent terminations can provide good insight into the quality of the management team. Ask to see documentation, exit interviews, etc. This can be quite enlightening and a good way to "see inside the organization."

This is also probably a good time to make sure there's an Employment Practices Liability Insurance (EPLI) policy in place. Buyers may ask to review any claims.

Confidentiality and Noncompete Agreements

Many companies have their employees sign confidentiality and noncompete agreements. Unfortunately, many times, these are either poorly written or because of state laws, unenforceable. If, as a buyer or a seller, you place value on these agreements, then they *all* need to be reviewed by an employment attorney. Emphasis is on the word *all*. I have found that in some cases these agreements have not been executed in a timely manner or modified on an individual employee level. If so, this may invalidate the agreement.

Union-Organizing Efforts

If you are part of, or talking with, a company that has one or more labor unions representing employees, then a basic review of the applicable contract(s) is a good idea. A general understanding of norms for the industry will help you evaluate the competiveness of the contract. It is probably unrealistic to think that you will be able to "bust" or break up the union. Instead you need to make sure you can work with the union and still be successful. Dig deeper if the company has a history where the employees have attempted to organize, even if unsuccessfully.

**

Sometimes the human resources of a company are neglected during a due diligence process. Sometimes the human resource is viewed as a commodity—static and easily replaced, much like the inventory in the warehouse. Individuals who run companies know better. They know that the employees—the HR—can be the trickiest part. Successful HR can be the most difficult to measure and unfortunately the most volatile and expensive if something goes wrong. A thorough due diligence process will involve a comprehensive look at the tactical and the strategic—the compliance and the best practices.

Jack Goldberg can be reached at (425-576-1900 or jack.goldberg@hrpmsi.com).

Chapter Eight

Playing poker–what's it worth?

Did you jump to this chapter right from the beginning? Good, because this is really what it's all about, isn't it?

As mentioned, as you plan your exit and the sale of your business, one of your first meetings should be with your financial advisor. It's important that you have a sound understanding of where you are financially as you prepare for your next great adventure in life. It doesn't matter if your goal is retirement, another business, acquisition or start-up, consulting, or just a couple years' hiatus.

Real-Life Story

One of my clients was planning for the sale of his business. His goal was to get enough for the business that when added to his current asset base there would be enough income generated to last forty years, as his wife was younger than him. His goal was income to last, under reasonable circumstances, until she was at least ninety.

He met with his advisor and got the impression that the numbers were "made to work" because the advisor saw a sizable amount of funds about to come under management. The seller was then referred to someone from a major life insurance company and, again, his impression was that the end goal was to sell product. He ended up with a fee-based planner who did not manage money or sell financial products.

Too many sellers go into the process blind. It's mandatory that you know what you need to make the rest of the process work and, if your business's value won't get you there at this time, what that value needs to be.

It's what you keep that's important

One key ingredient to the exercise of determining what you need is to know what you're going to keep after taxes and transaction fees. Later in this chapter we'll discuss terms and deal structure because there are different tax rates and various applications of those rates. For now, here are two examples.

Real-Life Story

The Wrong Way: The seller was burned out. Not from the day to day of the business but from the management of it. He had created a very successful service business and was the creative genius behind it. However, when it came time to sell, he lost all of his creativity. He was fixated on price; or should I say, a particular price, and didn't care how it was paid.

The buyer structured the deal with an employment agreement and a consulting contract. The net after tax to the seller was less than if he had taken a price of 15 percent less with proper deal structure.

The Right Way:* *Greg's deal was the opposite. His buyer showed him how he could accept an offer with a price 10 percent less than he wanted, get more cash (because the bank was willing to have a better loan package at a lower price), and have more money after tax than he would get at his asking price. Some of this was because of tax concessions the buyer made. However, those concessions got the buyer a better deal with about the same amount of after-tax acquisition debt payments. Most importantly, it got the buyer the deal on a very profitable and stable company (growth of the top and bottom lines every year during the Great Recession).

Who do you trust?

I'll say upfront that I don't have any certifications or designations in business appraisal or valuations and doing valuations is not the primary focus of my business. However, I have been around hundreds of deals and potential deals, and I do know the standard valuation methodologies.

But you have to watch out. I saw a backroom bank employee do a valuation for a buyer (and the bank) that was complete garbage. Why? Because he did not even try to understand the business or its financial statements and relied on very simplistic formulas, most of which were meaningless. It's important for anybody valuing a business to get a feel for the business beyond the numbers, because there are so many ways for a small business to reduce taxable earnings, accelerated depreciation disguises asset values and earnings, and the nonfinancial factors are a huge part of the process.

On the flip side, a client of mine had a valuation done by a well-known, well-respected, and experienced appraiser. His report came back with one-third of the value weighted on very optimistic projections. Of course, the business owner fixated on the total value in the report even though it was based on dynamic future growth. It had to be pointed out that banks don't use valuations with projections and that looking at the report without the projections gave a value of about 70 percent of the stated figure. (I said they were optimistic projections.)

My advice is to understand what you are getting and who you are getting it from if you get a valuation. Also realize that the balance sheet can play as important a part in the valuation as the income statement.

Real-Life Story

I titled this section, "Who do you trust?" for good reason. A business buyer client of mine hired an appraiser. We all got together to review the numbers, the methodologies used, and the discussion points with the seller. At one point the appraiser said that we would use a factor of "X" in one formula because my client was the buyer and we wanted the value to be low.

This wouldn't pass any industry standards or codes of ethics. In fact, it goes against such standards. As a seller, be careful if anybody suggests using factors to increase the value because you are the seller. This can easily backfire in the following circumstances:

- ***The bank won't finance the deal at that level.***
- ***The buyer's advisors see through the strategy.***
- ***The deal goes through but the buyer has trouble making the payments.***

A plethora of information

There are tons of books on small business valuation and many more articles that have appeared in business and trade magazines, not to mention everything on the Internet. One of the books I have uses the words *simple* and *easy* to describe its contents, yet it is filled with almost as many formulas as a college textbook.

Real-Life Story

On a "Partner" On-Call Network franchisee teleconference, we had one of our partners do a presentation on business valuations. This person had a financial background and some middle-market acquisition experience.

We followed along on an Excel spreadsheet as he discussed statistical analysis, standard deviations, and many other things I vaguely remembered from college math and statistics courses. When he was done, there was a stunned silence, unusual for this group of assertive people.

After what must have been ten or twelve seconds, I said, "Would you please explain what you said after your opening?" Following a bit of laughter, we got into a realistic discussion of how small businesses are valued.

One can face information overload and get tangled up in a process that is often exhausting. Realize that no matter what method, formula, or statistical analysis is used, it comes down to the fact that there are some generally accepted ranges where most deals happen. One of the best examples of this is a chart created by Rob Slee in conjunction with Pepperdine University and published in *Midas Managers*. Here is Mr. Slee's chart with the same information but in a different format.

Sales Range	Classification	EBITDA Multiple Range
Under $5 million	Small Businesses	2-3x
$5-150 million	Lower Middle-Market	4-7x
$150-500 million	Middle Middle-Market	8-9x
$500-1,000 million	Upper Middle Market	10-12x
Above $1 billion	Large Companies	>12x

Source: Copyright Rob T. Slee, 2007, all rights reserved.

Let's apply some common sense to the above chart and realize that there are exceptions. As stated previously, the larger the company, the greater the price, all other factors being equal. That means that a company doing $5 to 10 million in sales will sell for closer to four times EBITDA than a company doing $50 to 100 million in sales.

This book is for the business owner with a company in the lower-middle market and small business range on Mr. Slee's chart. If your firm is on the lower end of the lower-middle market range, don't focus on the high end of the multiple range, as it probably isn't applicable.

The 2014 Pepperdine University study on Private Capital deals states that the average multiple of EBITDA for companies with under $2 million of EBITDA is 4.2 and for companies with $2-5 million of EBITDA the average multiple is 5.1. Remember that these are averages and these figures are to be used as guidelines only. If you have great customer diversification, a solid management team and a lot of recurring revenue your selling price (and multiple) will be higher than a firm with the same EBITDA but with high customer concentration (risk), weak management and no recurring revenue (all bid work for example).

What do you really make (and what does it matter)?

Balance Sheet

There are many components to every business, and when it comes to valuation, using a quick multiple approach ignores the balance sheet, which is a mistake.

For valuation purposes, assets are divided into two classes. Essential assets are those necessary to deliver the product to the customer. They include inventory, furniture, fixtures, equipment, and vehicles (FFE&V). Without them you can't do business. They are generally included in the total value of the company.

Nonessential assets are necessary to having a business but not necessary to delivering the product to the customer. Common nonessential assets are cash and accounts receivable. Many businesses have little to no money in their bank accounts and can still deliver product. Many businesses have no accounts receivable and can still deliver their product (retail and restaurants are good examples).

Does the value of your essential assets matter? For inventory, definitely. You can't expect to get the same price for a company with a lot of dead inventory as you would a company with inventory that is 100 percent salable and that turns at or better than the industry average.

However, when it comes to FFE&V, there are two factors to consider.

What are the anticipated capital expenditures? In other words, what will a buyer have to spend to maintain the business at its current growth rate? If your assets are at the end of their lifespan, future cash flow will be less, all other things being equal, than if you have newer assets with a long projected life before replacement. Allowing for capital expenditures after determining EBITDA (or profit) gives a buyer a free cash flow figure, which is what will be available to pay the debt and taxes and fund growth.

With all of the constantly changing accelerated depreciation techniques available today, your book value of FFE&V is almost meaningless. What's important to a bank is the fair market value of these assets (actually, the bank may be more interested in the liquidation value). This is collateral and may affect the amount of the bank loan your buyer can get. But be careful in this area. Consult your CPA about depreciation recapture, which means part of the sales price will be taxed at ordinary income rates, not capital gains rates (in general terms, this comes into play if you allocate a value of an asset higher than its depreciated value on your balance sheet).

Income Statement

This is where the fun begins. It's rare to find a small business that has a tax return or income statement that accurately reflects the true profit of the company. One part of the reason is that there are tax techniques such as accelerated depreciation and amortization of goodwill (if you purchased the company and are still writing off the goodwill). The other big reason is that owners funnel nonbusiness expenses through the company.

Business owners should approach their bottom line, at least for three to five years prior to selling, as if they are in a contest to have the most profit and pay the most tax. However, that's tough for most owners. They either have a great aversion to paying taxes or their CPA takes it as his or her mission to reduce the client's taxable income by any means possible.

In the section on financial due diligence, I mentioned how it is considered fraud to not report income and to deduct personal expenses through the business. I don't recommend it, but it happens, and that is one reason it is common to "recast" or adjust the income statement to show the true profit and cash flow the buyer should expect.

The following chart is a simple tool to help you calculate your profit or cash flow that will be available to a buyer. Most of the categories are self-explanatory, but let's review some of them. First, realize that in an S corporation the owner often takes a low salary and high distribution, and in a C corporation it is the opposite. Therefore, we add back owner compensation to net income and deduct the fair market salary for the job being performed by the owner.

Category	2 Years Prior	Last Year
Net Income		
Owner salary		
Owner salary tax burden		
Excessive owner benefits (life insurance, etc.)		
Travel & Entertainment (not essential)		
Owner auto (not essential)		
Depreciation adjustment		
Amortization (of Goodwill)		
Interest (not continuing post-sale)		
Rent adjustment (that you over or under pay yourself for rent)		
Other		
Other		
Total		
Less: Fair market owner salary		
Less: Fair market owner tax burden		
Less: Anticipated capital expenditures		
Less: Other		
Total adjusted net profit/free cash flow		

Excessive owner benefits—If you have life insurance, deferred compensation, or a pension plan weighted in your favor, you can add these back to income. Do not add back standard medical benefits, similar to what all employees get and what the buyer will expect.

Not essential expenses—Do you deduct your car yet use it only to commute? Or perhaps you deduct your spouse's car (or your kids' cars)? What about that annual board meeting in Hawaii in January? These are not expenses essential to running the business. While the annual board meeting is legal, I recommend you consult with your CPA about auto expenses, other travel you write off, entertainment, and so on.

Depreciation—Work with your CPA to get a cost for anticipated capital expenditures and asset usage expense, which is really what depreciation is, other than all the acceleration techniques.

Interest and rent—If you have an acquisition loan, you should add back to income the interest on it. Realize that if you have a line of credit, the buyer will have a line of credit, and she will factor that cost into her calculations. Rent is adjusted only if you pay under or over market (usually if you also own the property) or if you expect the rent to change for the buyer.

There are too many businesses that have become "lifestyle" businesses for the owner. There's a blending of the personal and business checkbooks (talk to your CPA or attorney about any risks of "piercing the corporate veil" involved with this blending). Some CPAs are aggressive and tell their clients to write off anything and everything. Others are incredibly conservative and will question why your annual board meeting wasn't at your office.

For the sake of exit planning and selling your business, and as previously mentioned, realize that banks are increasingly suspicious when there's a long list of "add-backs" of personal expenses. Many bankers will discount these and thus reduce the cash flow they will use to calculate debt coverage ratios. Also remember the story I told about the owner who saved on taxes by running her household expenses through the business and lost out on four times the amount of taxes saved on the purchase price.

Real-Life Story

I have seen and heard just about everything when it comes to deducting personal expenses. The list includes the liquor store, Costco, the toy train store, Best Buy, shotgun shells, the cigar store, spouse cars, family cars, family salaries (for people not working at the company), the weekly grocery bill, vacations,

home remodels, and more. I once wrote a newsletter about an article in the* Minneapolis Star-Tribune *about a Twin Cities business owner who was put in jail for not reporting income and writing off things that make the above list seem tame.

I've had owners brag about the cash they skim, and one owner even asked me, dead serious, if I wanted to see the real books or the books he shows the IRS.

Many years ago a CPA told me he fired a client because of this type of manipulation. A CPA can lose his license if he knowingly signs a fraudulent tax return. He said he told his client that because the client owned a well-known and successful restaurant, lived in one of the nicest neighborhoods in town, and drove an exotic car, that he, the CPA, couldn't sign his tax return showing he made a minuscule amount of money.

Play it straight, maximize profits, pay taxes, and adjust your income for legitimate reasons. Your buyer and the bank will be glad you did.

The following is an article I wrote in 2013 on this subject. You'll notice some repetition with what I've written above and that's intentional.

AAA–Not to the Rescue

If the only way a buy-sell deal can be made to work is because of AAA, it's probably not worth doing. AAA stands for the following:

- Adjustments
- Assumptions
- Add-backs

In the world of privately held businesses, business owners' goal is often to pay as little tax as possible. When it comes time to sell, however, they want to demonstrate that the business has more cash flow than the tax returns (and financial statements) show. Often it gets to the point of ridiculousness; I once saw a seller state that $250 of lunches were personal, not business, and should be considered profit.

In my world it's common to adjust the financial statements so they look as if the seller was trying to win bragging rights for high profit instead of minimizing taxes. Some of these adjustments are easily justifiable, such as adjusting the owner's salary to market rate or if the seller owns the real estate and pays more than market rent. But they often seem to stretch the limits of sanity, and if that's the only way the deal can work, it probably isn't worth doing.

Let's look at the AAA of buy-sell deals.

Adjustments, as in, "you can adjust some of our operations to make more profit." I've seen where the seller or his representative stated that the employee pension contributions that are $150,000 per year could be reduced to $50,000 per year. This means another $100,000 of profit (and this makes the company worth more). Never mind that employees will absolutely "love" the new owner who has just slashed their benefits.

Similarly, I once saw a deal where it was stated that if the buyer reduced the sales staff's commissions from 10 percent to 8 percent, this adjustment would create more profit. Think slashing benefits will demoralize employees, try cutting their earnings and see how happy everybody is.

Assumptions, as in, "let's assume X happens and you'll make a lot more money." Examples include the following:

- We're assuming that gross profit will be 42 percent in the future (even though it's been 39 percent over the last five years and never more than 40 percent).

- The company has too much space. We're assuming the buyer can lease a smaller space at a lower rate (and who exactly is going to pay the exiting landlord for the rest of the lease's term?).

- There are too many employees, so our assumption is the buyer will let two people go, save that money, and therefore should value the business based on that higher amount of profit. In one situation, one of the seller's reasons for selling was that she was tired of working seventy to eighty hours a week. And the buyer is expected to reduce staff?

- We're assuming future growth at 12 percent a year for the next five years, so pay us more for the business now (even though it's been flat to 3 percent growth over the past five years).

All of the above are real-life examples of assumptions made to try and increase the price of a business.

Add-backs, as in, "we wrote off a lot of expenses on our taxes that really aren't related to the business (and, therefore, we've misled the IRS)." Now, some things are legitimate. A corporation can hold the annual meeting in Hawaii in January and write it off. It isn't illegal, but it isn't a necessary business expense either. Other add-backs border on the ridiculous. Here are some from a recent deal that didn't go through, one reason being the sellers wanted the price based on the following:

- Writing off personal Costco bills for all members of this multigeneration business

- Deducting gas, repairs, insurance, and more on all family members' personal vehicles

- Receiving the annual rebate from the distributor personally, not to the company (think that got reported on the 1040?)

- (Supposed) personal travel, meals, and other expenses at such a high amount it meant that nobody did much work between trips and other entertainment

To balance this, legitimate add-backs to profit could include the following:

- Life insurance on the seller
- Rent in excess of market (when the seller owns the building and will lease it for the lower market rate)
- Adjustments to depreciation with the recent high levels of section 179 deductions (as long as anticipated capital expenditures are factored in)
- Owner compensation to market rate (this could make profit higher or lower depending on how the seller pays himself)

AAA Conclusion

AAA in the world of driving a car is pretty cheap "insurance." And it truly can "save the day." (Excessive) AAA in the buy-sell world is akin to "putting lipstick on a pig." You can dress the business up, but if it takes adjustments, assumptions, and add-backs to make the deal work, it's the wrong deal. If it's (sorry for all the clichés) "the icing on the cake" that makes the deal great instead of just good there's no problem.

Cash flow terminology

Profit, EBITDA, SDE, ODI, recast income, free cash flow, and other terms bounce around the buy-sell industry like a racquetball in a fast-paced game. What's worse is that these terms are often defined differently. Let's take a look at them, what they really mean, and how to apply them. Because, no matter what, no matter how a valuation methodology is applied, it comes down to a return on investment (ROI), and using one term versus another can create drastically different results.

Profit—As written above, if businesses operated to maximize income instead of paying less in taxes, we'd get a truer picture of the income viability of a company. Small-business reporting is not like public company reporting where the public company wants to show maximum income to encourage an increase in stock price. For this reason the profit figure on the income statement or the tax return is rarely valid.

Recast profit—This is a much better indication of a company's status. It allows a buyer and a lender to know what the buyer's available cash will be. This is a very valid figure.

EBITDA—The acronym stands for "earnings before interest, taxes, depreciation, and amortization." This is supposed to give an indication of true cash flow because, in theory, depreciation and amortization are noncash expenses and interest is included because a buyer may have different financing than the current owner. However, EBITDA doesn't make allowances for Section 179 deductions, anticipated capital expenditures, or the cost of working capital, which for many businesses is a critical and needed expense. As with adjusted profit, you must allow for a fair market salary for the job of the owner. This is a corporate term, and you don't see public companies adjust and add back management salaries to profits.

Real-Life Story

For fun, Google "EBITDA and Warren Buffet." Here are a couple choice quotes from Mr. Buffet on the use of this term:

"You get depreciation by laying out money first—the worst kind of expense. It's the opposite of float, where you get money at the beginning and pay out at the end."

"References to EBITDA make us shudder. Too many investors focus on earnings before interest, taxes, depreciation, and amortization. That makes sense only if you think capital expenditures are funded by the tooth fairy."

Seller's Discretionary Earnings—This is often EBITDA plus owner's salary. The theory is that all money to an owner is discretionary and it's the owner's decision to take a salary, use the money to grow the business, or pay acquisition debt. I suspect it came about because brokers got sick of arguing about what the fair market salary for a business's owner should be. In reality, for most owners and buyers, a salary to support their personal life is not discretionary. An appraiser (and banker) would always allow for a fair market salary. In my opinion, this term is usually inappropriate and loses all effectiveness once a business's adjusted profit plus salary gets to $500,000.

Free cash flow—In simple terms, take EBITDA (including the adjusted profit figure that allows for a fair market owner salary) and deduct anticipated capital expenditures and operating interest (not acquisition interest). This is a figure equity groups and similar buyers often zero in on, especially in these days of complicated and changing accelerated depreciation schedules. It also gives a seller credit for recent capital expenditures that will reduce the buyer's need for capital expenditures.

A term that has come into vogue recently in middle market deals is "quality of earnings." In simple terms, if your profits, or their increase, are because of good management, an effective marketing campaign, or sustainable operational improvements, you have high quality of earnings. If your profits, or their increase, are from commodity price changes, dying products, or singular events, you have low quality of earnings.

Real-Life Story

A buyer reviewed a company's tax returns and said, "I like the business, but it's not making any money." The company was structured as a C corporation and the owner took a salary of about $750,000, which left only $50,000 to 100,000 on the net income line. Adjusting for a fair market salary gave a true adjusted profit figure in the $650,000 to 700,000 range.

Conversely, I've seen buyers get excited when they first look at an S corporation's tax return and see an inflated net income line because the owner was taking a salary of only $40,000 to 50,000.

Multiples

The above definitions are important to understand because, as previously stated, it all comes down to ROI. Your buyer, banker, appraiser, and you will all be concerned with the factor used as a multiple of earnings. The following example shows the differences, which are explained after the chart.

For this example, let's assume the company does about $5 million in sales, reports 10 percent profit before adjustments, and has a solid asset base that needs regular upgrading. For this example, we are assuming there are no serious red flags like high customer concentration, a tenuous lease that may require huge moving costs, or market factors that will negatively affect the industry. For simplicity's sake, I am assuming the nonessential assets are not included in this sample calculation.

Also, I'm assuming this is a manufacturing, distribution, or service business because retail and restaurant businesses have some additional factors and their multiple of earnings is often lower because of the higher (perceived) risk associated with those business types.

	Profit	EBITDA	SDE	Free cash flow
Reported profit	$500,000	$500,000	$500,000	$500,000
Adjustments	$100,000	$100,000	$100,000	$100,000
Depreciation		$100,000		$100,000
Operating interest		$50,000		$50,000
Owner salary			$150,000	
Capital expenditures				$50,000
Operating interest				-50,000
NET	**$600,000**	**$750,000**	**$900,000**	**$650,000**

Profit—Buyers for businesses in the $5 million range typically want a 20 to 25 percent ROI, which means a multiple of four to five. The multiple is lower for smaller businesses and can be higher for larger businesses. This gives us a price range of $2.4 to 3.0 million with a $2.7 million midpoint.

EBITDA—As we saw with Robb Slee's chart of EBITDA multiples, they increase as the business gets bigger. The same is true for the other factors. In Slee's chart we see that a $5 million business is on the border of a three and four multiple. This gives us a price range of $2.2 to 3.0 million with a $2.6 million midpoint.

Seller's Discretionary Earnings (SDE)—Your first inclination might be to use SDE, as it's a much higher number than the others. Of course, the generally accepted range of multiples is lower. Around the year 2000, I was recruited to join a prominent Seattle business brokerage firm. Typical deals were from $1 to 10 million in price and the firm had a great reputation. One thing that stuck out to me was that in the weekly meetings, when discussing possible listings (of only profitable companies) they always used a range of two to three times SDE. The potential listing agent usually argued for the high end and the others gave reasons why that wasn't realistic. Using this range, we get a price range of $1.8 to 2.7 million and a midpoint of $2.25 million on a company with $5 million in sales.

Free Cash Flow—You'll find free cash flow multiples to be similar to profit multiples, and they do grow as companies get to $10 million in sales and above. In this example, we get a price range of $2.6 to 3.2 million and a midpoint of $2.9 million.

	Profit	**EBITDA**	**SDE**	**Free cash flow**
Mid-point value	$2,700,000	$2,600,000	2,250,000	$2,900,000

You can see why I feel SDE loses importance as a business grows. The owner's salary becomes less relevant compared to the lower multiple range. The others are in a pretty tight range and then the influences become, as always, the nonfinancial factors, terms, relationships, and buyer and seller motivations.

I can tell you that some business brokers would read this and immediately argue with me that the range of multiples, the calculations, or other factors all give too low value. At the same time, buyer representatives, accountants, and others would tell me that the above is too optimistic.

As with any guidelines, use them only as such—guidelines. The explanation above is simplistic and presented to make a point. That point is that there are different ways to calculate earnings and different multiples for those methods. Buyers of $5 million businesses do want a 20 to 25 percent ROI; buyers of $15 to 50 million dollar businesses will lower that to about 15 percent ROI. There's enough evidence and history to show these are viable ranges, and these are the ranges necessary to allow for the risks of a small business (versus the risks a large public company faces and can handle).

Comparable sales

Historical sales information (i.e., comparable sales) is a little bit like the Bible. There is one Bible and many different interpretations. If a business is below average, the owner or selling team will point to average multiples as a way to increase the price.

As mentioned above, consider your use of average selling prices. I've had discussions with many people about the validity of (historical) average selling prices. Rarely will a business be average. Don't get caught in the trap of using averages as gospel.

Toby Tatum, certified business appraiser and the author of *Transaction Patterns* wrote my "Partner" On-Call Network associate Ted Leverette (in late 2011) and said, "Using a 3X multiple of seller's discretionary earnings for the vast majority of businesses represented in the Bizcomps database will tend to yield a value conclusion that is approximately double the correct amount." Or, a small percentage of good businesses are raising the average price of all the others. So be careful, asking too high a price may scare away good buyers.

> ***Real-Life Story***
>
> ***There weren't enough historical sales for the distribution company's SIC (Standard Industrial Classification) code so we looked at distribution companies in general at a size range that straddled this firm's size and eliminated all firms losing money. We noted the ratio of price to earnings (the multiple) and, just as important, the ratio of earnings to revenues.***

The firm had earnings 20 percent greater than the average (for example, if the average was 15 percent then this firm had 18 percent earnings). Our assumption became that this firm was an above-average firm and the justified price should be above average. This is just one way to use comparable sales information.

My advice to buyers and sellers is to not get hung up on comparable sales information. This is not a regulated market like real estate. Submissions to the databases are voluntary (as opposed to looking at the tax records) and there are no double checks on the information submitted. This information is really a guideline or rule of thumb and should be used accordingly.

We also don't know exactly what was included in the reported information. If two owners sell for five times profit and one keeps all the working capital and the other includes it in the deal, we have vastly different sales that are reported with the same price-to-earnings ratio.

Valuation methods

According to IRS revenue ruling 59–60:

> *The fair market value is the price at which the property would change hands between a willing buyer and a willing seller when the former is not under any compulsion to buy and the latter is not under any compulsion to sell, both parties having reasonable knowledge of relevant facts.*

Well, the IRS should have said hypothetical buyer, or hypothetical situation. Because never will the buyer and seller know the same things, perceive them the same way, or have the same motivations to do a deal now versus *maybe next year.*

This ruling covers a wide range of valuation methodologies, some appropriate and useful and some not. In the early 2000s the SBA came out with its list of approved methodologies. (I'm not sure if the SBA still adheres to that list, but it does now require appraisers to have a certification in order to do valuations on SBA program transactions.)

For example, the book value of a company is rarely reflective of the true worth, yet that is a method of valuation. Similarly, calculating the investment needed in a start-up to get to the place where the company being valued is (at this time) is not often valid. Both of these may be useful for unprofitable or new firms but don't have much relevance for a mature, profitable business.

In my world, there are three main methods with comparable sales used as a sanity check:

1. Capitalization of earnings

2. The IRS method

3. Discounted future cash flow

Research business valuations and you'll find a lot of appraisers talking about how there's as much art as science to it (and they're right).

Capitalization of earnings

For a small or midsized business, what are the most valid methodologies? Return on investment or capitalization of earnings is always at the top of the list. Every buyer wants a rate of return commensurate with the perceived risk of the business. This is why larger companies will sell for a higher multiple of earnings than smaller ones, all other factors being equal. Because there is less perceived risk.

In simple terms, the return on the investment is reflected by the price of the business. If the buyer desires, or demands, a return of 20 percent based on historical earnings, then he will pay five times earnings for the business.

The IRS method

As you might suppose, a method with the initials IRS in it will tend to lead to higher values, as the IRS often gets involved with gift and estate tax issues and wants a high value so there is more tax to collect.

In simple terms, the ongoing cost of the company's assets is deducted from earnings, and a multiple, based on the goodwill rankings on a one-to-six scale, are applied. This becomes the value of the goodwill and it is *added to* the value of the assets. Here's an example:

Earnings - $500,000	
Assets - $400,000	
Cost of funds - 10% (or an annual cost of $40,000 for the use of these assets)	
Average of Goodwill rankings – 4	
Profit	$500,000
Cost of assets	-$40,000
Net	$460,000
Multiple	4
Goodwill ($460,000X4)	$1,840,000
Value of assets	$400,000
Value of assets and goodwill	$2,240,000

Real-Life Story

The firm being sold was a high inventory business. In fact, the amount of their inventory was many times higher than similar firms because of shipping, the number of product variables (size, color, etc.), and production lead times. Using the IRS method gave a value so high that no buyer would pay it. The return on investment would be way too low for this $5 to 10 million (sales) company.

The company was getting a very poor return on assets, and because of this its value wasn't much more than the total value of the assets. In this case, growth was the answer. At twice its size, the firm projected it would need the same inventory with a better inventory turn rate.

Discounted Future Cash Flow

It's often said that buyers buy because of potential and pay based on history. This method determines a price based on future projected earnings. Personally, I think buyers and sellers should be very careful of this method or any variation of it, and I'm not the only one. The SBA will not allow a valuation that uses projections of any type. The value has to be determined based on historical earnings.

In simple terms, the projected earnings have a discount rate applied to them to create a present value of those earnings. This sounds fine in theory, but just imagine the situation if someone bought a company in 2008 based on all the rosy projections floating around. Nobody imagined the Great Recession. As a seller, you don't want to be dragged into a lawsuit because you sold based on projections that didn't come true, whether it's the buyer's fault, the economy, or anything else.

Real-Life Story

A client showed me two valuations done on his firm. The first was from a national road-show company that sold incredibly expensive valuation reports and was known for inflated values in those reports. The value was so high that this owner just laughed because he knew that, even in his wildest dreams, no buyer would pay that amount. They got these high values by basing them on projected earnings.

The second valuation was from a very reputable regional CPA firm. They used the same method (discounted future earnings) and added in a residual value. This means that they projected the buyer would sell the business in five years, discounted to a net present value the price the buyer would receive, and added it to the current value (based on projections). In other words, pay the seller now for what you will sell it for in the future. Their value was even higher than the national firm's value.

Again, the risk is a future lawsuit if those projections don't materialize. This client was smart enough to know that he wouldn't buy his own business for these inflated prices and no sane buyer would either.

Goodwill ratings

I've used the term "goodwill" numerous times and every buyer, seller, and every banker should want a lot of goodwill. It means the company is getting a great ROI on its assets. Some bankers, and unsophisticated buyers, will often call it "blue sky." Some bankers refer to it as an "air ball," meaning it might not have any value because it isn't collateral they can attach to. My feeling is that goodwill is valid, it's a number based on profits. Blue sky is on top of goodwill and is based on unrealized potential.

The following is a standard form used by business appraisers to estimate the feelings of company owners or buyers on the goodwill of the firm. You can find it in many places (perhaps with some slight variations).

I instruct clients to "rate your company and be honest," to give thought to each category, and put down the number they feel is most representative of the company's status. *Ratings do not need to be whole numbers and can range from 0 to 6 (for example, they could be 3.1, 4.7, 1.4, or 5.0).*

Give serious thought to your answers and justify them. Question why you chose a particular number versus the one above or below. For example, if a rating is a 4, why is it not 4.5 or 5, and why is it not 3.5 or 3?

Please provide a brief explanation of why you chose each rating. Be skeptical of any ratings at the 5 or 6 level. It is highly unusual for a business to be at a 5 or 6 in any of these areas. A score at this level means your firm is in the "best of the best" category. Provide *proof* of why you're at this level.

Alternatively, if you rate yourself a 1 or 2 in any category, please give a brief explanation of why you don't think you're "up to speed" in that area.

Risk Rating______
0 - Continuity of income is uncertain
3 - Steady income likely
6 - Growing income assured

Competitive Rating______
0 - Highly competitive in unstable market
3 - Normal competitive conditions
6 - Little competition in market; high cost of entry

Industry Rating______
0 - Declining industry
3 - Industry growing faster than inflation
6 - Dynamic industry; rapid growth likely

Company Rating______
0 - Recent start-up or not established
3 - Well established with satisfactory environment
6 - Long record of profitable operation and excellent reputation

Company Growth Rating______
0 - Business has been declining
3 - Steady growth, slightly faster than inflation
6 - Dynamic growth rate

Desirability Rating______

0 - No "prestige" status; rough, dirty, undesirable work

3 - Respected type of business in good environment

6 - Great demand by people desiring to own this type of business

TOTAL RATING______

These ratings serve two purposes. First, they provide insight into the buyer's and seller's feelings about the company, its future, and the risk involved.

Second, in the IRS valuation method, the average of these ratings is used to determine the multiple (for this method).

Don't ignore the balance sheet

While it's true that most deals have a price (and value) based more on cash flow than assets, don't ignore the balance sheet. In these days of complicated accelerated depreciation, it pays to have a CPA unravel the balance sheet.

A company with very low assets will tend to sell for a lower multiple of earnings than a company with a lot of assets, all other things being equal. There is a feeling of safety with assets and less goodwill. Remember the Five Cs of banking—one of them is collateral.

My first look at a balance sheet is to see what the quick ratio situation is. The quick ratio is cash and equivalents and accounts receivable versus current liabilities. I take it one step further and look at the quick assets to all liabilities. In other words, if the business sold, could the seller pay off her debts from the current cash and receivables? This is often a deal point, especially if the seller owes more than she can pay off from her assets.

Real-Life Story

The owner had an accounting background. He didn't just show me a balance sheet, which had assets after depreciation of under $50,000. He had a list of assets with cost, date of purchase, depreciation, estimated useful life, and his estimate of the current fair market value. The current value of assets was about $750,000 (of which a bank may use half toward collateral). This shows how Section 179, immediate write-off of assets purchased, and other techniques can skew a balance sheet and why I recommend an accountant undo the depreciation schedules to get a true current market value.

A recent trend is for working capital to, more and more, stay in the company. This has always been the case in larger deals, and is now working its way down the deal size ladder. You can't build a company with an involved balance sheet and expect to unravel it at time of selling (or at the time of valuation). In simple terms, as in my story, have an appreciation for your balance sheet because buyers, bankers, and appraisers will.

So what stays with the company? My feelings are that if you're selling someone a very small business, with a price of $250 to 500,000, you're going to keep all the cash and A/R and pay off all the bills. But when the value of the company gets above $1 million and especially $2 to 10 million or more, then the buyer is truly buying a business (not a job), and part of the business is the working capital.

The following explanation is from attorney Walt Maas with Karr Tuttle in Seattle. Walt is one of the top Mergers and Acquisition (M&A) attorneys in the Northwest and offered this insight recently to a mutual client.

> It's customary for transactions to be cash free/debt free with a working capital adjuster that uses average Trailing Twelve Months (TTM) end working capital (generally A/R plus inventory, less A/P

and accrued liabilities, but excluding in each case cash and current portion of any debt) as a target or PEG amount.

Closing date actual working capital, as so calculated, is then compared to the target working capital and the seller is paid the delta if closing working capital is higher than the target (theory is that seller has invested incremental cash to the extent of the excess and should be repaid that amount by buyer) or buyer is given a price reduction if closing working capital is less than the target (theory is that seller has liquidated working capital below the average and, as seller retains cash, should repay the delta to buyer by way of a price reduction).

The idea is that the TTM average, with the adjustments described above, is the amount of working capital at closing necessary to run the business.

Using a working capital adjuster also polices the management of working capital by seller prior to closing (i.e., no benefit to the seller of accelerating A/R or delaying payment of A/P as a means of generating retained cash) and provides a backstop to your working capital diligence by means of a postclosing true up process to determine actual working capital at closing.

Walt Maas can be reached at 206-223-1313 or wmaas@karrtuttle.com

Terms and Deal Structure

Terms won't influence a valuation, but they will influence the price. As a seller, you need to look at the whole package, including buyer capabilities, cash at closing, net after tax, and what you will do with your money. In 2014 and preceding years, interest rates have been at all-time lows. In 2009 one seller went to his buyer, who he felt was the right person to take the business to the next level (he was right), and renegotiated to carry a larger note. His note was at 6 percent interest and he said he couldn't come close to that with the bank.

When it comes to structure, this is where your CPA earns his fee. His job is to keep you out of trouble, which means for you to get as much of the price at capital gains tax rates versus ordinary income rates as possible. In an asset purchase, this means not having any depreciation recapture (putting the value of the assets above what they are on your books) because this is taxed as ordinary income. Again, consult your CPA in advance and at the time of the deal.

Myths of Business Valuation

Here are some myths of valuation and pricing I've come up with over the years.

The "rule of thumb" says my business is worth X. Rules of thumb are just that and nothing more. They give an indication but do not substitute for a valuation. Use them for quick comparisons only. Here's a big reason why: often a rule of thumb is an average. If one company sells for 2X revenue and another for 1X revenue, the rule may state companies in that industry sell for 1.5X revenue (a simple average). If you use this "rule," you could tremendously shortchange yourself.

I'm going to sell my small, privately owned company for the same price to earnings (P-E) ratio as a large, publicly traded company. Not valid for at least two reasons. Public company P-E ratios are based on after-tax profit. Private companies are valued based on pretax profit (one reason being that small business owners have access to a wide variety of tax avoidance strategies). Second, as stated previously, the larger the firm, the less perceived risk and the higher the multiple.

Owner's compensation is profit. Profit is what is left after allowing for fair market compensation for doing the job of company president.

I deserve something for my sweat equity. There is no such thing as sweat equity. Sorry, but no sane person is going to overpay for a business just because you put in a lot of effort to get it where it is. Profit over a manager's fair market salary is your payment for sweat equity.

The business is worth the current market value of the assets. I've had buyers tell me they won't pay for blue sky (goodwill) and my response is then they probably won't buy a business because more businesses are valued based on cash flow. I've also had naive CPAs tell their clients nobody will pay more than book value for their company.

There is a value to the cash I pocket (without reporting on my taxes). If you're willing to cheat the IRS, how much trust should a business buyer have in you? If you're skimming, you've already been paid for it by not paying taxes.

The price needs to cover the personal and business debt I owe. Many years ago a seller informed me that he set the price by adding the business debt, personal debt, and the price of a new RV. Stop laughing. I'm serious. In 2011 I heard a similar story from the owner of a multimillion-dollar sales business (which was struggling).

The losses and my reduced salary over the last three years are a fluke. Just look at the profit eight years ago. In 2011 the owner of a business told me what he wanted, I told him I thought he'd be lucky to get half of what he wanted, and he said his rationale was that in 2006–07 he made a lot of money and business would be back to that level in another year or two so he should get paid based on that profit level.

Valuation standards

While many people who do business valuations are not certified or members of a valuation professional group, they should adhere to industry group standards. Go to the following websites to see the standards from two industry groups, the National Association of Certified Valuators and Analysts (www.nacva.com) and the Institute of Business Appraisers (www.go-iba.org).

Common sense is always appropriate

A few pages back I told the story of an appraiser who said he was using one formula versus another because he was working for the buyer not the seller. Not only is this not ethical, it doesn't pass the common sense test. Why would either party to a transaction (or the seller, if the work is for planning purposes) want a product that is not done right?

The fact that you are reading this book and have made it this far means you most likely own a profitable business (not one you want to unload on the "greater fool" who is willing to pay for potential). I'll also assume this is not the first time you have encountered the subjects of business valuation, selling a business, or getting a deal done.

Ask yourself, what would I pay for a business like mine? That's what a good buyer is going to pay. You wouldn't overpay for the opportunity to maximize the business's potential, and you wouldn't want to create ill will by trying to get a steal. A deal has to work for both sides. It has to be win-win, and all of the valuation methodologies, commonly accepted ranges of value, and myths to avoid allow you to get to that point.

If you want to get working on some things to increase the value of your business, start with this list of twenty reasons why a buyer will think your business is worth less than you do.

1. **Dependency on owner**—Too many businesses suffer from the all-controlling owner who not only knows how to do everything but also insists on being part of everything. Don't let yourself be the bottleneck. Buyers may pass or offer a lower amount when they see how big the shoes they have to fill are.

2. **Customer concentration**—No buyer wants there to be a small number of key customers doing a disproportionate share of your volume. Diversify your customer base and realize if you have a highly concentrated customer (or industry) base, you may be asked to include an erosion clause that lowers the price if a top customer leaves.

3. **Financial statements and tax returns differ**—There isn't much to say about this. Have good accounting systems and safeguards and accurate statements. Don't rely on too many adjustments for the tax return or an overwhelming amount of add-backs (to profit).

4. **Dependency on a key employee**—A company recently had severe problems when its top salesperson left and took most of his accounts. This problem could manifest itself with a technical expert, machine operator, or office manager who knows how everything in the firm works.

5. **Poor lease or no lease available**—You may think a month-to-month arrangement is great as it offers flexibility. Buyers and banks think about how expensive it is to move. In fact, for anything other than a professional-type business (like consulting, accounting, etc.), your buyer won't get a bank for longer than the term of the lease including options. Too short of a lease means too short of a seller and/or bank loan and too high payments to make the deal feasible.

6. **Behind the curve on technology**—While some people will think this is an advantage to a buyer to do things more efficiently, in reality there is a cost to hardware, software, and implementation. Use your experience of your business to get technology up to speed, show increased efficiencies (and profits), and sell for a higher price.

7. **Skimming cash**—There isn't a CPA around who will let a buyer be convinced to pay a price based on unreported cash. First, you are cheating the IRS. Second, is it worse that you're skimming or worse that you say you are but really aren't?

8. **Too small**—A business doing $2 million in sales will not get the same multiple of profits as a similar business doing $20 million. There's just more risk factors the smaller the business is. A major disruption to a small firm is a minor hiccup to a larger firm.

9. **You are blending too many personal expenses into the business**—Yes, there are advantages to paying for things with pretax dollars instead of after-tax dollars like employees have to. Carry it too far and it's almost as bad as skimming. Bottom line, buyers and banks like to see profits. Show a lot of profit, pay some tax, and it will come back to you in multiples when you sell (and make it easier to sell and finance the business).

10. **You have to work too hard in the business**—Buyers look for businesses they can work *on* not work *in*. They may not have your passion for your product or service; instead they have business skills to leverage what you've done. Get out of the business of doing things an employee could do.

11. **Financing is hard to get**—Banks don't like your industry, business, or acquisitions in your industry. If your industry requires a high level of industry experience, a buyer without that experience won't get an acquisition loan. However, you may get a higher price by financing more of the deal.

12. **No business or marketing plan**—While a plan may not directly reduce the value of your firm (other than the fact that companies with a plan have significantly higher profits), a business and marketing plan may add to the price a buyer is willing to pay.

13. **Poor or no management team**—Buyers like to manage and lead; they don't like to do. A poor team means a lower value.

14. **Salary is not profit**—An appraiser will want to know the fair market salary for the job of running the company. If you weren't there, you'd have to pay someone to be president and that salary is not profit (by a long shot).

15. **Saturation**—This is often a function of franchising or low barriers to entry. Eventually this leads to competition based on price, and it's hard to win in that situation.

16. **Special skills or license needed**—About two-thirds of all small businesses need an owner with general business skills and business common sense. Those are the types buyers like the most. If you have to be a PhD in an advanced scientific field to own the business, well, good luck finding someone with money who wants to own a business.

17. **Vendor concentration**—Don't overlook this. The vendor(s) may not pull any tricks, but what happens if your sole source has problems or goes out of business?

18. **Working capital needs**—You pay your people this week; you pay your suppliers in thirty days; the rent and other overhead every month; and your customers pay you in ninety days. That's working capital, and that's why fast growth can be a problem. It takes cash to grow, and if you don't have access to enough cash, you've hit a bottleneck (see the first reason on this list).

19. **You have a job and it's not as CEO**—In other words, you work *in* the business, not *on* the business. If the business can't survive if you're not on the shop floor, you aren't a manager, you're a working employee. This probably means growth is stagnant as you have no plan, leadership, or management.

20. **You've bled the business**—Every last cent goes into your take-home pay and the assets are in need of repair or replacement. This leads to lower profits. One owner was so cheap he wouldn't buy a new printer. After the sale, the buyer bought a new printer, the accounting department's systems stopped freezing up when something printed, and efficiency soared.

Chapter Nine

Going for the close

In chapter one I twice used the term "logical buyer." Make sure you know how logical buyers fit into your goals and their options for funding. Your goal is not to focus in on any particular logical buyers, but rather to eliminate those who aren't a fit while keeping your options as wide and varied as possible.

For example, if your business is doing $3 million in annual sales, you are not going to sell to a private equity group. Conversely, if you're doing $33 million in sales, chances are you are too big to sell to an individual buyer. So, prepare for the logical buyer(s).

Selling, recapitalizing or a liquidity event

Before you do, make sure you know what you want out of a deal. By that I mean there are options other than selling the business and walking away ninety days later. Consider these before preparing for various buyer types.

Sell 100 percent

You can usually sell 100 percent of the business and be gone in ninety days to one year, depending on the size of your business and your role (the less dependent the business is on you, the sooner you can leave). If you're doing under $10 million in sales, this is usually the best, and often only, option. Even from $10 to 20 million in sales, depending on the level of your profits, this will be one of your best options. The corporate executive who has honed her skills and built up her capital working for others wants to be in complete control.

Real-Life Example

There are reasons deals don't work. One of the top reasons is the seller stays and works at the company, full time, part time, or as a commission salesperson. It is extremely tough for someone who has called the shots for many years to work for someone else. All it takes is the seller saying something like, "That's not the way we've always done it here," with a sarcastic tone to get the employees wondering if the buyer really knows what he's doing.

This is much more of a risk if you're selling to an individual financial buyer. My advice is that if you sell to an individual, sell it and move on.

Recapitalization

Once you hit a certain size, you have the option to sell part of the company with (perhaps) some of the money going to you and most, if not all, going into the business to reduce debt or for working capital. At the point where it becomes tough for an owner to fully capitalize the business, this may make sense. You are betting that owning a portion of the business that can dramatically scale is a better option than owning 100 percent of what you have.

You may be asked to stay on, to either run the company or be part of the management team. Although a business that takes advantage of this option is larger than the companies in the above Real-Life Example, you face some of the same control, or lack of control, issues. Make sure you're ready for this.

Liquidity event

For you, this is similar to recapitalization, although all the money goes to you. Whether you sell 20 percent or 80 percent, you get the money. The question is, who will purchase less than 100 percent of the company, and especially, who will purchase a minority position? To have this option, you'll need some scale and a management team and be willing to stay on and not be in full control anymore.

The Selling Process

In chapter two we discussed growing by acquisition and presented a nine-step process to make an acquisition. Here's an eleven-step process for selling; you'll notice many items are exactly the same, as they well should be. The buyer and seller should be working together to get a deal done—it becomes a team effort, especially if you adhere to the following:

1. Preparation

2. Who will sell it for you

3. Identifying the logical buyers

4. Marketing the business

5. Screening buyers

6. Finance, value, and price

7. Deal-making

8. Negotiation

9. Due diligence and contracts

10. Closing

11. Transition planning

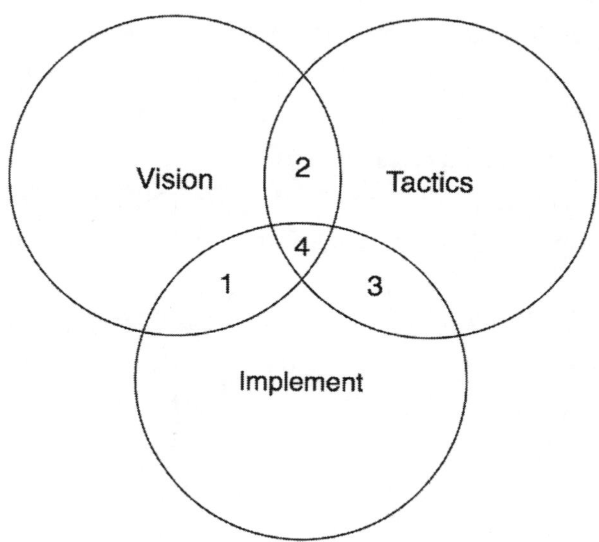

The above diagram shows that when exiting your business, you need strategy, tactics, and implementation. Pay attention to the following:

- Strategy and implementation without good tactics leads to ineffectiveness.

- Strategy and tactics without implementation means you're stagnant.

- Implementing tactics with no clear-cut strategy has you wandering.

- All three together mean a successful exit (with style, grace, and more money).

Let's concentrate mainly on the steps not previously covered. When it comes to the last six steps, just switch your focus from being a buyer to being a seller.

Preparation

This is what the majority of this book is about, so I won't spend much time here. Preparation means determining your financial needs, what you'll do if you sell, and the process of growing and preparing the business to maximize value. One of the most important questions to answer is "What is the business worth?" We covered it previously, and yet all of that info just gets you on the right course. It will help you to constantly monitor where you are. If in doubt, an independent business appraiser can help you on this.

One thing I didn't mention in the previous chapter has to do with a warning when it comes to third parties valuing your business. Never, and I mean never, pay anybody to value your business who also wants to sell your business (a broker). There is an inherent conflict of interest, as the broker may want to inflate the value to get the listing.

Real-Life Stories

A business broker told an owner he could get him eight times EBITDA for the business. This was for a $10 million manufacturing business with much lower than industry average gross profit, a low net profit, and no proprietary product. Who was he kidding? Not this owner, as he saw through it and told the broker where to go.

The CPA told the owner his business was worth the net value of the assets. Never mind that this business had solid profits. This conservative CPA didn't understand valuation and just looked at the balance sheet.

The attorney and CPA told the owners that their small business was worth five times income. The owners figured that included profit plus both the husband and wife's salary. Another intermediary and I consulted on this and told them it was worth about 40 percent of their estimate. It also hurt the company that the business was extremely dependent on the husband.

The point of these three stories is to be cautious and use common sense.

Who will sell it for you?

This is one of the most important decisions you can make. My advice is to think this through and not concentrate simply on the costs. A good intermediary will generate multiple buyers and should get an increased price that more than covers his fee. Even if he doesn't, the emotional savings you get may be worth it.

Let's look at your options.

You

You can always do it yourself; this works best if you have a buyer in hand. You're a smart person, you own a business, and you are doing well—probably because you've taught your team well and they're productive. And, you'll save the fee. By all means use your selling team, whether it includes an intermediary or not. Your odds of success increase dramatically and your emotional rollercoaster will be leveled out.

Searching for a buyer can be laborious, and you have a business to run. You'll have to have thick skin and not take things personally. This is doubly important if you're marketing the firm (not just working with one buyer) because the buyers you meet on the public market are often unsophisticated. They'll make outrageous demands and won't understand the process, valuation, or much else about business buy-sell. They can waste your time and frustrate you no end.

Look at all aspects of this before deciding to do it yourself, consult with your advisors, get referrals (if they have to cold call you or use direct mail, they're probably not very experienced), and interview a few intermediaries. The distractions of a buyer search can easily reduce profits to the amount of a selling fee.

Broker or Investment Banker

I define a business broker as someone who lists and sells small businesses. An investment banker is similar but works with larger companies, usually middle-market firms, and also helps with securing debt, recapitalizations, and other financial transactions. For now, let's use the term intermediary for both.

The benefits to using an intermediary are numerous and include the following seven reasons:

1. **Confidentiality**—The biggest issue with 98 percent of sellers is "Will anybody find out I'm for sale, especially my customers, employees, and vendors?" An intermediary can protect that confidentiality a lot easier than you can. Because if you talk to anybody about the fact you're selling, they know you're for sale. An intermediary can disguise the business, insist on a nondisclosure agreement, and not share any information with unqualified buyers.

2. **Marketing**—An experienced intermediary will have a database of qualified buyers to contact first. Your business may never have to appear on the Internet sites with all the junk. Part of the marketing process is screening, so that you don't waste time meeting tire kickers or unqualified buyers.

3. **Time**—As in the time you get to spend running your business, not marketing your business. Yes, you will put in more time than expected working with buyers, but this is miniscule compared to the marketing function.

4. **Pricing**—The previous chapter described different valuation techniques. Someone involved in the market on a day-to-day basis will be able to best guide you through the maze of methodologies, formulas, and the real world. As mentioned in the previous Real-Life Story, use some common sense and don't fall for a valuation that sounds too good to be true (just to get the listing).

5. **Negotiations**—Do you want to wear the black hat and be the tough negotiator with someone you'll be working with for quite a while and probably receiving payments from for years? It's both time and emotion (it's hard to not take things personally). An intermediary will often keep you above the fray. You may never hear some of the things a buyer says, and the buyer won't hear your emotional outbursts.

6. **Deal structure**—This is different than price and includes payment terms, tax structure, when money goes into escrow, all the "little" conditions that make it a deal, and more.

7. **Closing**—This is the goal, isn't it? Your intermediary is your guide. She will provide you with education, direction, and feedback. The "administrivia" from signed letter of intent (LOI) to closing frustrates most sellers. "Why does the buyer/bank/attorney need that information?" Just as importantly, she will guide the buyer through the process and prevent analysis-paralysis.

Real-Life Story

Many advisors who don't work regularly on transactions don't understand the details. A CPA once said he didn't understand why his client needed to provide written lists for the purchase and sale agreement. Let's assume this is a list of customers for one of the schedules. He said, "He [the seller] has already told the buyer that information." True, and once the list becomes part of the contract, the seller is representing and warranting that those are the company's customers. In other words, the seller is guaranteeing he's done business with those customers. And this applies to all similar information for schedules.

Consultant

Since the Great Recession, I've seen a lot more nonintermediaries offering businesses for sale, usually for their existing consulting or financial services clients. Some do a decent job and some (most) leave a lot to be desired. They often don't understand the process, how to screen buyers, or the market. I just ran into one of these situations, the pricing of the business was way off and the advisor's justification for the price was based on an article written by a professor at a school in Africa. Unbelievable! Does this person think he's doing his client a favor?

If you have a close advisor and she offers to help sell your business, I recommend you vet her the same as you would anybody else, making sure she has enough experience to do a good job for you, which is a lot more than being a friend.

Remember, whoever is marketing and selling your business has to be a good salesperson. He has to research the market, actively prospect, and nurture the process.

Identifying the Logical Buyers

This chapter started by giving a rough example based on whether you're doing $3 or 33 million in sales. Part of your team's job is to identify to whom not to market. This has to do with your company's size, product, location, growth capabilities, and management team. Take some time to ponder this, as it will save you time, money, and angst.

Marketing the Business

There are volumes written on this, all different. The most important part is to find prospective buyers. You may have everything else down pat, but if there are no buyers, what good is the rest? It's like having a salesperson who is super in front of customers but who has no customers to call on. His in-person skills are useless.

There are proven ways to market your business, including networking, directly contacting potential buyers, and advertising, most of which is via Internet listing sites these days. The latter is the least effective, as you or your intermediary will have to screen dozens of dreamers to get to one or two serious and qualified buyers. The smaller the business, the more appropriate advertising is.

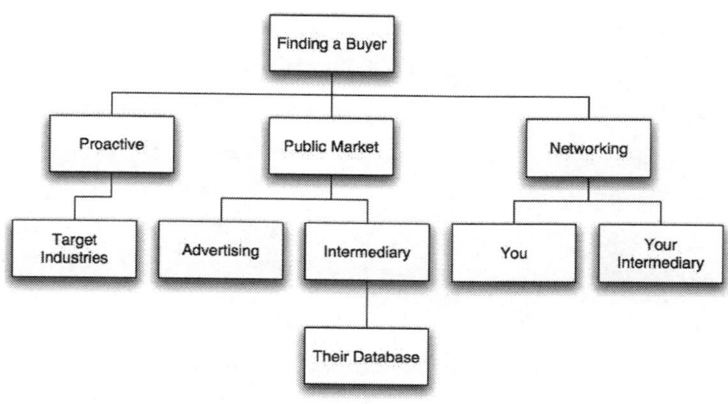

What buyers want to see is a good overview of the business. Intermediaries usually do a good job on this. They're experienced in putting together a book (also called a prospectus or memorandum) on the business. The more qualified and high level your buyer is, the more she will expect a good book that explains the business.

All buyers, especially high-level ones, will discount any fluff, especially if it involves the use of the word *potential.* If you're going to talk about potential and growth, be able to back it up. Not in your book, but in person with buyers. It is most important that you delineate to the buyer *exactly what your competitive advantage is and how you will leverage that competitive advantage to grow the company.* I've seen more good buyers walk away from deals (they maybe shouldn't have walked away from) because the seller couldn't articulate the growth strategy than for any other reason.

Real-Life Story

Two high-powered buyers (a team) were discussing a business opportunity with two sellers. This was a business doing about $15 million in sales, 30 percent gross profit, a high net profit, about 85 employees, and a good fit for the buyers.

After the meeting the buyers decided to pass on the business because they got the feeling that the business was a commodity, was tied to the owners, and had no perceivable growth strategy.

Some of their impressions were true, some not. The owners were too integral to the business, but they were going to stay as minority owners, so that shouldn't have been an issue. Their product/service was not truly a commodity. So, it came down to growth.

The sellers admitted after the meeting that they didn't handle it well. When I asked one of them about the value proposition, I received a clear answer delivered forcefully. Why they couldn't do it with the buyers, I don't know. Let's hope they learned from it.

Your memorandum should describe the business, its products, services, people, customer types, certifications, processes, and so on. Basic financial information should include at least three years of income statements and balance sheets. A cash flow statement helps but is not necessary at this time. Be careful with the AAA mentioned in chapter eight; don't go overboard.

One area that generates mixed reactions in the intermediary community is the use of projections. Often I see projections up to seven years but don't look past year two. In these fast-moving times it's tough to project more than one year.

I also know intermediaries that refuse to do any projections; they leave that to the buyer. They are worried about liability in case a buyer sues if those projections aren't met.

This latter point brings up a related issue about intermediaries. Some will delve deep into your business so they can understand it and explain it to buyers. Others take a hands-off approach and simply play matchmaker and salesperson. I don't think there's a right or wrong, but in any case they should ask you a lot of due diligence questions so they're not surprised later.

Screening Buyers

This is one of the most time-consuming parts, and the smaller your business, the more buyers you will probably have to screen. As mentioned before, the three qualifications for a buyer are the right experience and skills for the business, enough capital, and a good personality. Start with the latter, and if you build a relationship, ask for background information (most of which is on LinkedIn anyway) and a financial statement.

Then it becomes tricky, as you're trying to determine if the potential buyer is a good fit for your business. If yes, you're going to be "selling" him on your value and finding out if he's willing to part with his money (for your business). The relationship is key. I've seen buyers who've been the only one talking to the seller—even with listed businesses—because the relationship was so tight (and often, because of the relationship, it was the only business the buyer was pursuing).

So what are you looking for to eliminate a buyer? Here's a good starting list; the first few are killers, the others are red flags:

- Poor relationship
- No trust
- Not financially qualified (ask in a first meeting or call, ask for proof in a second meeting)
- Limited or no management experience
- Uses the term "air ball" to discuss goodwill
- Talks negatively about any part of your business (a sure sign of a bottom feeder)
- Jumps too soon into financials, your "secret sauce" for growth, etc.
- Starts talking about price (very) early in the discussion (asking you is OK, giving parameters without knowing too much is a concern)

This is an extremely time-consuming process. If you run into a good buyer on your own, great; if you have to do a search for a buyer, it could become your half-time job.

Finance, Value, and Price

This is pretty well covered in the previous chapters, so I'll just offer a few tips here:

- If your deal is under $10 million, the bank may use the SBA program. This means you'll get up to 90 percent in cash at closing.
- In all cases where a bank is involved, your seller note will be subordinate to the bank, either partially or fully.

- There's a difference between the multiple range for middle-market companies and small businesses. Don't let anybody con you into thinking he can get a much higher price than normal for your size range. He can't.

- It's not just what you get paid, it's what you keep and if you get paid in full (your note). Even a small hassle can disrupt your life, so a lower price to a great buyer is better than a higher price to a mediocre buyer.

- Don't take it personally if someone offers less than you want or think it's worth. This is business.

- Earn-outs need a valid reason for existence. For you to get more than it's worth or for a buyer to shift some of the operational risk to you are not good reasons.

Real-Life Story

My first reaction to a business I was introduced to was that it was worth no more than $3 million. The reply I received was that the valuation was about 20 percent higher.

After going through the valuation in detail, a few flaws were found. One I remember was that the appraiser made an assumption that the manufacturer's rep firm could be let go and those sales brought in-house at an annual savings of $150,000.

Once these "flaws" were validated, expectations changed, and the business ended up selling for $2.5 million. As in a lot of things, valuations are garbage in–garbage out. Be careful the input is correct, because your buyer will.

Deal-Making

This is where art overtakes science. If you're doing this yourself, be careful as tenseness abounds and even a casual comment that is misunderstood can have huge negative ramifications. One role an intermediary can perform very well is to wear the black hat, say the tough things, and be a protective shield for both sides.

While everybody says they want a win-win deal, everybody also wants the most for him or herself. Deal creep can run rampant here, meaning one party or both is always asking for a little more. Once it's received, there's another request until the other side is so irritated they're threatening to walk away. Even if you don't use an intermediary, have someone (a professional) you can vent with.

Contrary to common thought, the most important factors in getting a deal done are not price, terms, and conditions; they're tactical. The strategic factors are as follows:

Motivation—Nothing will happen if both parties aren't motivated. We'll assume you are selling for reasons other than trying to get someone to grossly overpay you. You have to screen buyers thoroughly to determine their motivation. The individual buyer with a lot of money and a big, fat, and secure paycheck is not as motivated as the executive who just lost her job. The company with a hole in its product line that you fill is a lot more motivated than the company firing on all cylinders.

Relationship—This is the key to all deals. You have to like the buyer. After all, he's going to run "your" company and take care of "your" employees and "your" customers.

Real-Life Stories

By the time I had a celebratory lunch with Jim, we had sold the company he'd started to a competitor, and he had bought two businesses. As we discussed relationships, he said something I'll never forget: "I would never buy from or sell to someone I didn't like." This should be the mantra for all buyers and sellers.

Rob didn't buy into the "relationship thing" as he called it. That's why it took him much longer than other buyers during a vibrant market. His style was to ask for financial statements and the business's "secret sauce" within twenty minutes of meeting the owner. No wonder some of them said thanks but no thanks and called me to say they wanted to sell but not to him. The good news is he finally met a seller with a personality just like his, who I believe had trouble getting buyers interested in his company.

Education—You've read this book so you have an understanding of the process, valuation theory, how to behave, and more. Assume most buyers don't have this knowledge, so your advisors or you will have to educate them.

All parties will get frustrated; there are common valuation ranges and it's a process of give and take. In addition, you'll be performing due diligence on the buyer, not just the buyer on your company. And finally, there will be some buyer and seller remorse, so expect a deal to get done when both sides are a bit unhappy.

Eventually it does get to price, terms, and conditions. If there's not a similar philosophy on price, there will never be a deal. If either side feels pressured on price, they'll find a way to kill the deal. It's when you're close that posturing stops and negotiating begins.

Negotiation

In my first real job after college, I was involved with some union negotiations. Not the most pleasurable thing to do, and I constantly reminded myself that most buy-sell negotiations are pretty tame compared to union negotiations, and the parties have to remain friends or the deal will die.

As mentioned above, there's usually give and take. The only time there's not is when one party is smitten with the other (buyer or seller fever). So what really gets negotiated? Price often comes first and terms follow. If there's a bank involved, the bank often sets many of the payment parameters, so both sides must understand the bank conditions.

Some common negotiated items include the following:

- **Working capital**—How much is needed? How is it calculated? If inventory's involved, is it usable and salable? Banks love it when the deal includes adequate working capital, and you should too; it helps assure buyer success. One of my appraiser friends tells me that he always figures 10 to 12 percent of annual sales should stay in the company as net working capital and I think this is a good guideline, as is the explanation from Walt Maas in the previous chapter.

- **Work in process**—This should be on the income statement as a current liability for costs in excess of billings and a current liability for deposits. You'd think that would make it simple, but it doesn't always. On one recent deal, we agreed that the seller would make the margin on the amount of deposits and the buyer on the remainder of the billing.

- **Seller note**—A seller note is the part of the deal that you finance. It's your "skin in the game," which banks and buyers want. With the SBA's newer rules (as of 2013–14) it's opened this up to negotiation. It's a lot different from when the bank told the seller he'd get the same terms as the bank and that was it.

- **Earn-out**—An earn-out is when part of the price, or additional price, is contingent on future performance. Your CPA and attorney will scream when they hear there's an earn-out, and they'll tell you that you'll never see one dollar of it. That's overreacting. Especially if there's a good reason for one. Good reasons for an earn-out include that you have a new product line that hasn't been exploited yet, or you have huge dependencies, like extremely high customer concentration, product domination, or one employee has too much responsibility. Bad reasons are that the seller wants more than it's worth, or the buyer wants to pay the fair market price only if the business grows (transferring risk to the seller). Also, as of this writing, the SBA does not allow earn-outs with business acquisition loans.

Three final tips:

1. You have to stay friendly with the buyer, as you'll be working together for months or longer.

2. Never let the attorneys get involved with negotiations, especially on business issues. This is a deal killer.

3. Trust your team and use them in order to keep your emotions in check.

Due Diligence and Contracts

If your intermediary, accountant, or attorney doesn't tell you this (and even if she does), realize that the administrivia of due diligence and the purchase and sale agreement will drive you nuts. No matter how prepared you are for it, you'll be overwhelmed by the requests for information from the buyer, bank, accountants, and attorneys. There's no way around it; it's a fact of buy-sell life. See Appendix G for the things a buyer must do. You may have to assist with some of these things also.

The appendices are filled with just about every due diligence question you could be asked, other than the little things specific to your business. You may use these questions in an acquisition or a mock due diligence, and if you don't, at least study them so you're prepared.

In addition, Appendix E is a list of current bank requests for an SBA loan and Appendix F is a sample list of what might be asked if an asset audit is requested. The bank often needs an asset audit if accounts receivable and inventory are a large part of the collateral. On occasion the bank may ask for a valuation of FFE&V. A buyer probably won't ask for this last item, but will be more interested in useful life, replacement cost, and other anticipated capital expenditures.

The easiest way to share the information is to set up a Dropbox folder or similar, put information in the folders, and invite the relevant parties to the folder. You can have different folders for your team, the buyer, the bank, and so on.

As mentioned, the purchase and sale agreement is another area that will drive you nuts. The buyer's attorney will probably draft the agreement and list of schedules. Hopefully the attorney is experienced in buy-sell transactions the size of your deal. The brother-in-law who's a family lawyer is as bad as having an attorney accustomed to $50 million deals drafting a contract on a $5 million deal.

Real-Life Story

It was about a $2 million deal and the buyer's attorney sent over a fifty-five-page agreement, plus schedules. To the credit of the seller's law firm, they declined to read it and drafted an appropriate agreement.

I asked the buyer about his attorney and the overkill on the agreement. As he raved about this attorney, he mentioned that his attorney had recently worked a deal where the buyer was the CEO of a company involved with an acquisition in France. What is appropriate for international, middle-market deals can be excess for $2 million (and even much larger) deals.

Purchase and sale agreements can be reasonable and at the same time give both buyer and seller the protections they need. Here are a few insights:

- Representations and warranties are where both parties "guarantee" what they are stating is true and correct.

- The buyer's attorney will want the reps and warranties to state they are on behalf of the seller and seller shareholder (or seller member if it's an LLC). The seller's attorney will try to get the term "seller shareholder" removed, usually without success, because all the seller has to do is dissolve the corporation and it can make the reps and warranties almost useless.

- The schedules are where you list things you are representing and warranting. This could include customer lists, assets, orders, inventory, contracts, license and royalty agreements, and just about anything you are saying contributes to the business's value.

- Both attorneys will want the other party to state unequivocally that he represents and warranties things. Both will want their own client to state, "*To the best of my knowledge* I represent and warranty…" (This is an attorney game.)

- You will subordinate your note to any bank note. Don't let your attorney or anyone else tell you to get this removed. It won't happen. If you want a lot of cash at closing, and the buyer needs a bank to get you that cash, then you will accept the bank clauses and subordinate.

Real-Life Tip

Your buyer, like (almost) all buyers, will be overwhelmed with information. He may ask the same questions more than once, and that's not a sign of inability or stupidity. He may be testing you. He may ask about a subject more than once, in a slightly different way, to see if you give the same answer. Or, the "drinking from a fire hose" syndrome has hit him and some things just floated away from his flooded brain.

Appendix H has a master list of schedules from my friend Greg Russell with PRK Law in Bellevue, WA.

Closing

This is what everybody is waiting for, right? It's the big day and the start of your next great adventure in life, with a sizable chunk of money in your bank account.

Sometimes all the final documents are signed in a formal ceremony in a lawyer's office or the escrow attorney's office. Other times documents are signed separately, scanned, and e-mailed to the closing attorney. When signed at the actual closing, there are rarely contingencies. A lot of the timing depends on your relationship with the buyer and your attorney's preference.

Other times, the final papers are signed a week or two before closing with contingencies for the buyer meeting the employees, customers, or vendors. Meeting the employees is the most common contingency, and unless the employees walk out en masse, the deal is on. (It's never been an issue in my deals.)

The closing attorney, often an independent escrow person, will prepare a statement for both buyer and seller. The buyer tells her how much money to wire to the escrow account and will account for her down payment, costs for things like lien checks, taxes due, escrow fee, and so on. Your statement will show the gross funds you'll be receiving and deductions for your costs, which may include intermediary commission, escrow fee, and the like.

The money from the buyer and the bank goes into escrow and the buyer and seller will sign "escrow instructions." Those instructions to the escrow agent determine when the money will be wired to you. There may be no contingencies and the money will be wired once all funds have cleared into the account. It may require the buyer waiving contingencies, as mentioned above, clearance of liens, bank approval that all debts are paid, or something else.

Timeline to Closing—Appendix D has a timeline courtesy of my friend Altchech at ACT Capital Advisors in Bellevue, Washington. While most of the activities on the list are the buyer's responsibility, you have to provide the information. This is where getting overwhelmed by administrivia hits.

The timeline here is simply a sample and has many of the tasks and steps needed, especially if an SBA bank loan is used. I recommend your buyer and you use this, and modify it for your deal, as it keeps everybody on the same page.

Transition Planning

This is one of the most overlooked areas in the buy-sell process. Both sides get so involved with everything needed to close that postclosing day one buyer and seller look at each other and say, "Now what?" You can help the buyer and yourself tremendously by making sure you have a plan for at least the first week or two. While this preparation happens preclosing, it takes place postclosing. There's a lot more on this subject in chapter ten.

Whew! It's over. It drove you nuts, but it was worth it. Take a deep breath, celebrate, and do your best to help the buyer be successful.

Chapter Ten

Life after selling

Let's go full circle from Chapter one and discuss what you're going to do now that you're no longer a business owner (assuming you're not on a long-term contract, still have equity, or have something else keeping you there).

Mike had a passion for semitrailers and even in his sixties he became a part-time truck driver. Greg loved boats; he refurbished them, cruised, and just generally loved anything to do with boats. David started a new business. Gary had a hobby farm with livestock, chickens, and more and became quite involved with it. There's no right or wrong as long as you do some planning sooner versus later.

Transition Plan

Ask yourself, in your business, what are the five most important things the buyer needs to know and accomplish sooner rather than later? Write these down. Then do it for the next five and so on. This is a great starting place. The list will include much of the following:

- **Sales**—Products, customers, industry and competition, value proposition, and key selling tactics

- **Finance**—Systems, procedures, reports, inventory management, and who does what

- **Human resources**—Management team, key employees, culture, procedures, policy manual, and who does HR (the owner shouldn't)

- **Operations**—This will vary by industry, but don't forget to train the buyer on customer service

- **Growth**—The plan, tactics, competitive advantage; what's worked, what hasn't worked, and why, etc.

Some initial transition tactics that have worked well include the following:

- The buyer hosts an introductory lunch, gets to meet the employees, discusses his plans, and, most importantly, lets the employees know he's not making any changes—especially with staff, so they should realize their jobs are secure.

- A day-by-day schedule with a little bit of everything for the buyer.

- The buyer shadows you the first few days, just to see what you do and have the opportunity to ask questions and observe operations.

- The seller plans a short vacation, maybe three to five days, two to three weeks into the transition. This lets the employees know things are OK without you there.

Below is a sample transition and training plan that a (very detailed) buyer put together. It's overly ambitious and probably wasn't adhered to because there's still a business to run, but it outlines very well how this subject should be approached. You want to get out in whatever time the agreement specifies, so the more organized the buyer and you are, the better off you'll be.

Strategic Transition and Training Plan

This is a sample only. Your buyer's plan may look nothing like this. This was for a sales, installation, and service company.

Before Close:

- Continue building the business plan.
- Continue to gather information and learn the industry.
- Ensure corporate affairs are in order.
- Establish financial and banking account relationships (all the things on the closing checklist).

First Thirty Days:

- Review any operating plans, performance, and personnel data.
- Meet with employees one on one and ask how they see the business improving.
- Assess how things are going and where you can add value.
- What are the challenges and opportunities?
- Do you still need the seller around?

Thirty to Sixty Days:

Discuss preliminary findings with the seller (after thirty days). What are the key issues?

- Culture
- Sales effort
- Restructure duties
- Team capabilities; are changes needed?
- Customer relationships
- Vendor relationships
- Other
- Do you still need the seller around?

Sixty to Ninety Days:

- By this time you should have a good understanding of the business.
- Where should you focus your efforts? Sales, operations, growth, culture?
- What is the seller's role in the future (consult, disappear)?

Training Plan–Tactical

The following table outlines a tactical training schedule of items to consider on a weekly basis. (This is for the first week only, which is why I said this plan is overly ambitious.) The buyer should provide this to you, get your input, and get you to agree to it.

Week 1

Sales

- Review basic sales strategy (leads, follow-up, etc.).
- Spend time with the salespeople as they call on customers. How are leads generated? What is their style and approach?
- Get up to speed on all products.
- Schedule introductions to suppliers and vendor training.
- Visit a few local customers (don't plan the major sales training this week).
- Plan major sales calls for next week.

Operations

- Listen to and begin answering phone calls.
- Figure out the scheduling system.
- Determine how jobs are bid and how the software is used.
- Visit a job in progress.
- Schedule time to spend with each technician.
- Spend time with key people if available.
- Determine what type of network is set up, if any, and reconfigure if necessary.

Accounting

- Establish a new company in the accounting system.
- Sit with the bookkeeper to learn exactly what she does.
- Download all information on company policies.
- Set up outside payroll services.
- Apply for fleet fuel cards and company credit cards.
- Visit CPA to finalize company setup.
- Ensure online bank account software and hardware for remote deposits is set up and working.

HR

- Review any and all employee records.
- Download all system documentation.
- Gather remaining signatures needed for corporate docs.
- Finalize team member assessments and their capabilities.
- Ensure all licensing with state L&I/Employment security is transferred.

Goals

By the end of week one you will have:

- A general understanding of how the sales process works in this business.

- Observed live sales calls.
- Ensured everyone is enrolled in new benefit plans as applicable.
- A general understanding of all products and services the business offers.
- The new accounting system up and running.
- Established payroll procedures.
- Been introduced either by phone or in person to key stakeholders or have meetings scheduled.
- Installed remote access systems to allow you to access the system from home.

Your job is to help the buyer achieve so much success that she can pay off your note ahead of schedule. During the deal phase it may have seemed that you were adversaries. Now you're teammates with common goals. To get you out of there, have the business thrive and everyone be wildly happy.

Your rights post-sale

Let's assume you are not the buyer's landlord—that's a completely different subject with different rules. We should assume you are a seller involved with transition, a note holder, and possibly an employee or contractor to the business.

If you sold the company and received all cash at closing (rare, but it happens), you don't have any rights and don't need any. It's like when you buy a house. On day one you can repaint or remodel any way you want and the seller has no say in the matter.

Let's assume you are holding a seller note. In most cases you'll have similar rights as a bank and you'll want to make sure these rights are detailed in your note. Normally this means you'll get timely financial statements (monthly, quarterly, or annually). The bank will have its debt coverage ratios and similar, and you'll tag along on those (and be in a subordinated position).

What you won't have is any say in how the business is run. Even with a note. A note is a form of legal tender, and if you sold 100 percent of the company, it's considered payment. Be prepared for this; it's why you need to screen buyers carefully and have a solid relationship.

For a legal perspective on this, here's an article from Michelle Bomberger with Equinox Business Law Group in Bellevue, WA.

The Deal Is Done–What Are Your Rights?

As a business owner selling your business, it's always a relief when the documents are signed and the check is written—the deal is done! However, there are a number of things to keep on your radar in the months following the closing to protect your rights.

1. **Payment Obligations—Promissory Note**—In most transactions, the buyer has an ongoing obligation to pay the seller some portion of the purchase price through a promissory note. As the creditor, you should know the terms of the promissory note, such as the payment date and payment amount. More importantly, you should know what constitutes a default and what notices you are required to give the buyer with respect to payment. If you don't follow the notices defined in the promissory note, you may lose time in trying to collect or obtain a default judgment against the buyer. You may also have a personal guarantee by the owners of the buyer, which typically gives you the right to pursue those guarantors immediately upon default by the buyer—you don't have to wait for all collections efforts against the buyer to pursue the guarantors. For this reason, you should have a plan for how

and who you must communicate with to enforce your rights as a creditor of the buyer and any guarantors.

2. **Payment Obligations—Earn-Out**—Many deals contain an "earn-out" provision where the seller is paid over time based on certain results of the company after the buyer takes control. Usually the buyer is required to provide regular reporting on company performance and make payment when certain dates or milestones are achieved. You should be proactive in obtaining these reports and ask questions early on. You do not want to wait months before realizing you have not received reports or payments on time or that there have been significant errors in reporting or calculations. The transaction documents likely have an "audit" function as well that you may invoke if you feel the figures are not accurate. The buyer's failure to provide reports or accurate data doesn't affect your right to obtain your payment, but the longer you wait, the higher the chances of not getting paid.

3. **Representations and Warranties**—The transaction documents list a number of "representations and warranties" made by the buyer. These are statements where the buyer promises certain facts. If you find that any of these statements are false, the buyer may have breached the agreement. Depending on the nature and severity of the breach, you may have claims against the buyer for money damages or even to terminate the deal. Most sellers don't want to reclaim the company or roll back the transaction—but the right response depends a lot on the specific circumstances.

4. **Ongoing Involvement—Employee**—As the seller, you may be asked to stay involved with the company as an

employee beyond the closing. In doing so, you should have an employment agreement that outlines the terms of your continued role. Remember an employment relationship is often "at will" meaning that you can be terminated at any time. If your compensation as an employee is really a part of the price of the transaction, you should make sure your job is protected and you cannot be terminated except in certain specific circumstances and that you have a mandatory severance package if you are terminated otherwise. In this situation, you are subject to the employment laws, which may trump the intent of the transaction documents.

5. **Ongoing Involvement—Consultant**—Instead of staying on as an employee, you may have an ongoing relationship as a consultant. The consulting agreement describes your obligations to work for the buyer and the buyer's obligations to pay you. As a consultant, you have the right to be paid for the services rendered, so you should be sure the terms you describe match what you're willing to perform. The language should ensure you are paid in accordance with the transaction terms and that the agreement cannot be terminated unilaterally by the buyer without compensation.

You should be aware of your rights following the closing and ensure the transaction documents properly address these rights. With these in place, you can move quickly upon any foreseeable issues and enforce your rights before these issues get out of hand, avoiding the potential loss of some of the purchase price or incurring expensive litigation costs.

Michelle Bomberger can be reached at (425-250-0205 or michelle@equinoxbusinesslaw.com)

To finish, here are my twenty rules of exiting and selling a business:

1. Searching for a buyer is sales; it's the same as when you prospect for customers. There has to be a good fit and the buyer must add value (like you do for your customers).

2. Cash is king (and so is cash flow). The more cash flow you have, the higher your price and the more cash you'll get at closing.

3. The queen is relationships, and like in chess, the queen is the most powerful piece in the game. It's a relationship game and don't forget it; nobody buys from or sells to someone he doesn't like.

4. It's not what you get; it's what you keep. Pay attention to taxes, terms, and structure.

5. Watch out for dependencies in the business. The first place a buyer looks for dependencies is at the owner. How dependent is the business on you?

6. You must show confidence, speed, creativity, and constant innovation.

7. Growth hides a lot of operational warts, and those warts tend to work their way out.

8. Make it so the buyer falls in love with the business model and its value proposition (not just the product). This means build a business with a defensible competitive advantage and leverage your competitive advantage to grow.

9. The bigger the spreadsheet, the less chance of a deal. Don't let the buyer get analysis-paralysis.

10. There are no perfect deals, so don't get emotional because the deal isn't perfect. Emotions cause more angst than anything else.

11. What makes you a good business owner can make you a bad deal person.

12. Terms are often more important than price.

13. Don't fall for valuation traps and simplistic formulas. Don't believe that because a $400 million company sold for ten times EBITDA that your small business will also sell in that range.

14. Due diligence is for proving what you've told the buyer during analysis; it is not time for surprises. Don't forget to do due diligence on your buyer and do it sooner rather than later.

15. Understand that the buyer and the bank will be "nosy" and the administrivia near closing will drive you nuts but must be done.

16. Have a great advisory team and use them. Don't try to do legal, tax, or related work yourself. It's not worth it and you're likely to make a mistake (and those mistakes can haunt you).

17. Don't let your buyer get overleveraged. Too much debt will come back to haunt the buyer and you.

18. You both will make a leap of faith. Do it right and that leap is off a chair, not the roof.

19. The only thing worse than no deal is a bad deal. Be patient and make sure the buyer is a great match.

20. Don't run a lifestyle business (meaning don't blend your business and personal checkbooks). Take some time, prepare the finances, marketing, and all of your systems, and you'll maximize value.

Appendices

Appendix A

Master Due Diligence List

You'll use this if you grow by acquisition, perform a mock due diligence on your company, or to prepare for buyers. Start by establishing responsibilities and a time line.

LEGAL DOCUMENTS

- Is the corporation (or LLC) in good standing?
- Articles of incorporation
- Foreign jurisdictions
- Officers/directors/owners
- Subsidiaries and/or affiliates
- Special shareholder rights (i.e., preemptive rights or other agreements)
- Minutes of board meetings (three years)

- By-laws
- What capital has been invested or loaned to the business?
- How has the company been capitalized until now?

COMPANY'S BUSINESS

- Describe the nature of the business
- Describe each line of products and services sold
- Describe proposed emphasis and direction of business
- Is there an intention to widen the range of products and services sold?
- Are there any limitations to products, tariffs, licenses, copyrights, etc.?
- Intellectual property—trademarks, trade names, copyrights, patents, software, trade secrets, other
- The method of sales, contracts with suppliers
- Contracts with other companies, etc.
- Are subcontractors used and for what?
- Are there any long-term contracts with subcontractors, etc.?
- A list of competitors and a description of their products

- What do you know about the competitors' financing and technical resources?

- In detail, what is the ease or difficulty of entering this business?

- Description of distribution channels

INDUSTRY GROWTH

- What is the estimated growth rate of the industry in the next five years?

- What factors will affect growth in the future?

- Are prices industry-wide stable or increasing?

MARKETING STRATEGY

- What are the marketing objectives?

- How will the objectives be implemented?

- What marketing effort is required?

- What expense is projected?

MARKETING PLAN

- Who and how many people are involved in marketing?

- What are historical sales increases/decreases by line (percentages)?

- Sales projections by product, percentage of future revenue

PRODUCT PRICING

- How are products and services priced?
- Will there be any price changes in the future?
- How does pricing compare with competitive and comparable products?
- Review actual invoices with major customers (to check for discounts, special deals, etc.)

CUSTOMER ANALYSIS

- Who are the customers?
- What are the trends in this customer group?
- Customer list by volume of sales (three years)
- What is the procedure to sell products and services?
- Copies of all client agreements or contracts
- What will be the determining factors to a buying decision?
- Do a few high-priced, well-connected salespeople control sales?

FACILITIES REQUIRED

- What facilities changes will be required in the future? Include size, description
- Technology requirements, hardware, software, licensing agreements, etc.

EMPLOYEES

- List of officers and directors (and key employees)
- Resumes of officers and directors (and key employees)
- List of all employees—salary, date of hire, and title
- Copies of employment agreements
- Employee turnover, out of ordinary?
- Compensation schedule for owners, officers, and key employees (including bonus plan)

DUE DILIGENCE LIST

- List of shareholders and percentage ownership
- Company's attorney, CPA, insurance broker, health insurance broker, etc.
- Company's bank and statements, deposit books, check register, QuickBooks file, etc.
- Environmental reports
- Employee manuals
- Copies of company leases
- List of all major assets—current, at fair market value
- Brochures and other marketing materials

- Financial statements for the last five years
- Financial statements, monthly for one or two years
- Accounts receivable aging report
- List of all debts and liabilities
- Copies of the last five years' federal income tax returns (4506 with IRS if needed)
- Copies of three to five years of state sales and use tax returns
- Copies of all agreements, loan agreements, notes, pledge agreements, and security
- Copies of all profit-sharing or deferred compensation plans
- Business plan
- Litigation history and anticipated (both ways), court search
- Insurance coverage, any changes, etc.
- Liens (equipment, tax, etc.)
- Off-balance-sheet items, vacation, sick pay, etc., and proprietary information such as drawings, reverse engineered and manufactured parts, etc.

Appendix B
Non-financial due diligence questions

ORGANIZATION

1. Organization chart including current and projected operating management

2. Managerial positions to be filled or eliminated

3. Employee roster sorted by function (job description) and location showing:

    - Compensation (base, bonus, etc.)

    - Bio of key employees

4. Employment agreements, noncompete agreements, and severance agreements

5. Employee turnover statistics

6. Historical use of consultants and outsourced "employees"

7. Availability of qualified personnel

8. Copy of employee benefit plan(s)

9. Overview of your company's present or former pension plans

10. Vacation and sick-leave policy (paid; rollover if unused?)

11. HR policies and procedures

12. Labor/employee relations and union issues (if any)

13. Written policies and procedures, operations manual

14. Kinds and amounts of insurance for the business and on the owners, costs

15. Claims filed during past five years

16. Contact info for your insurance agents. How has each helped you tailor your insurance to the needs of the business?

17. Copyrights, trademarks, service marks, patents

18. License and royalty agreements

CUSTOMERS

19. How many active customers do you have?

20. What percent of your total annual volume is done with your largest customer?

21. How many of your customers represent 5 percent or more of your business?

22. How many customers does it take to make up 25 percent of your total sales?

23. Of the major customers (the ones identified above) you did business with over the previous two years ago, how many are not "active" customers? Why?

24. Please characterize your relationship with your customers.

25. Please characterize, in general, your perception of your customers' satisfaction with your business.

26. Describe a time when you really came through for a customer and she let you know.

27. Describe a time when you let a customer down and she let you know.

28. How do you handle dissatisfied customers? What kind of warranty do you provide?

29. Do you know of any customers who are planning to leave or are putting their business "out to bid?" If so, who are they?

30. Customer satisfaction surveys usually concentrate on the areas listed below. Rate how you think your customers evaluate your company (one is low, ten is high).

Products	**Service and Support**	**Delivery and Timeliness**
	Ordering and Billing	**Employees**

Rating (1–10)

An alternative to a customer satisfaction survey is to have somebody call as a reference check: "I'm thinking of doing business with [Company Name] and hoping you can tell me what it's like working with them." Open-ended questions work best as they allow the reference to expand without limitations, and it doesn't sound like an interview or interrogation. Just treat it as if you were asking for a reference or if you are being a reference.

EMPLOYEES

31. Please characterize your relationship with your employees.

32. How would your employees describe your relationship with them?

33. How many employees have been fired or quit in each of the last two years? What were the reasons?

34. Describe the quality and competence of your workforce. How would you characterize the morale?

35. Which, if any, employees do you think or have told you they are planning to terminate their employment?

36. How difficult is it to find good replacements or additions to your workforce in the various skill levels?

37. Where do you find replacements? Newspaper, walk-in, word-of-mouth, referral, etc.?

38. How many employees do you have? What are their positions and titles? How long has each employee been employed by you? What do the key employees do on a daily, weekly, and monthly basis? (Provide detail about their job descriptions.)

39. How much is each employee paid? How is that determined? Do you think this is high, low, or average for your industry and geographic location?

40. Are employee policies and procedures documented? Explain.

41. What does the owner do on a daily, weekly, and monthly basis? Be as detailed as possible. What skills would your replacement need to have to successfully run this business?

LANDLORD

42. Do you have a written lease?

43. What are the terms of the lease, including the *specific* terms of an option to renew or extend?

44. Are you willing to help a buyer obtain an assignment of the lease or, if necessary, negotiate a new lease?

45. Please characterize the relationship you and other tenants have with the landlord.

46. What is the going rate for similar space "down the street"? What about "across the street"?

BANKING AND LENDERS

47. Where does your business bank? Describe your relationship with the bank.

48. What is the name and title of the bank employee you confide in?

49. Describe the line of credit (and other lending relationship) you have with the bank. Is the bank of sufficient size to grow with your company?

50. Will you go with a buyer to your bank for the purpose of assigning/obtaining credit for the business?

51. Describe the relationship you have with other sources of financing (i.e., leasing firms, factors, etc.)

SUPPLIERS/VENDORS

52. Characterize the quality of your relationship with your suppliers.

53. Describe how prices are set (i.e., price list, bid, etc.) and the credit terms they extend you. Are these terms competitive? Are you aware of any planned or proposed changes? Are there enough suppliers to keep them competitive?

54. Are you willing, at the appropriate time, to introduce a buyer to your key suppliers and help the buyer secure similar pricing and terms? How likely is it to occur?

55. Are any of your vendors talking about discontinuing lines, materially changing their products or the way they do business? If so, which vendors and what changes are they proposing?

ADVISORS

56. What is the name and contact info of your attorney and CPA? Identify any business consultants you use or have used in the past few years.

57. Please characterize your relationship with your advisors.

58. How would each of the above describe their relationship with you and your company?

MARKETING AND COMPETITION

59. What characterizes your competitive advantage(s)?

60. What is your current and forecast market share by customer group and/or product group for your company and, to the best of your knowledge, for each of your major competitors?

61. How do you price your product, and how do you track product costs (cost of goods sold)?

62. What are your credit policies for customers and employees?

63. How do you advertise and promote your business? What does the program cost? How do you evaluate the return? What is the return typically? Is there any reason you know of why the advertising and promotion activity should change?

64. What methods do you employ to obtain and retain customers?

65. What is the typical sales cycle (from lead to sale)?

66. Who are your major competitors? What are their strengths and weaknesses?

67. How is your product different from theirs? Do you compete mainly on price, service, or quality?

68. What is the most immediate threat or potential vulnerability of your business caused by your competitors?

69. What is the health of your customers' industry?

70. Is the business subject to seasonal or economic cycles? How so and to what extent?

71. What strategies do you employ to take advantage of or minimize such impacts?

72. Identify major customers you lost within the past three years? Why?

OPERATIONS AND REPORTING

73. What government agencies regulate your company? Please describe your relationship with those agencies.

74. How often do you prepare a written business plan or budget? Is your most recent plan/budget available for review? If not, why not?

75. Describe the financial recordkeeping process, including the relationship with your CPA. Is your accounting procedure documented?

76. What other kinds of recordkeeping systems do you have? For example, personnel, production, quality assurance, customer complaints, etc. Are they documented?

77. How often do you generate financial and other reports that measure the performance of your company? How old is the data contained in these reports when you get them?

TECHNOLOGY

78. Describe your computer systems. How they are used and who primarily does what on them?

79. What software do you use? Is any of it proprietary?

80. Are all the copies legal and registered?

81. Who develops and maintains your website, what are the costs, and how do you feel about the service?

82. Answer the same for your web hosting. When does your hosting agreement expire? When do your domain name registrations expire?

83. What type of Internet access do you and your employees have at work? What speed (TI, cable, DSL, etc.)?

84. Have you had any virus or security issues? What antivirus and spyware software do you use and is it up to date?

85. What operating systems are you running?

86. When was your computer equipment purchased?

87. What additional hardware or software would improve business operations, efficiencies, or profits? What is the cost for these improvements?

88. Are there any other technology issues I should know about?

OWNERS

89. Please list all the shareholders/investors in the business and the percentage each of them owns.

90. What are your reasons for selling your business?

91. How will you train the buyer to operate your business?

92. Would you like to be involved in the business after the sale? As a consultant? An employee? Full or part time?

93. What are you planning to do after the sale?

94. What is the nature of your other business interests that relate to this business?

GENERAL

95. Has the business ever been involved in a lawsuit? If so, what was the nature and outcome of each major case?

96. Describe legal action that you think might be threatened or pending against the company.

97. What amount of annual capital spending is required to allow the business to remain competitive?

98. Have you received from any party a written report that states a fair market value for your business or a price fairness opinion for the purpose of offering your company for sale? If so, when? Provide a copy of the report(s), memorandum, etc.

99. Describe any information that you know of that has not been disclosed by you that might have a bearing on the viability and/or the valuation of the business.

Appendix C

Rate Yourself on a One-to-Ten Scale

1. I've reduced or eliminated any dependency the company has on me, the owner.

2. We regularly invest in our assets (there are no looming large capital expenditures).

3. We have great financial systems, they produce accurate financial statements, and we have and use a good management report system.

4. We work on innovation (moving forward) as opposed to problem solving (fixing something back to standard).

5. We've developed a solid management team.

6. We regularly learn from our people who are the point of customer contact.

7. We have and implement a growth strategy.

8. We know the greatest opportunity we have in the near future.

9. I don't use my business as an extension of my personal checkbook.

10. We have great credit and access to funds as needed.

11. I know how to get the most out of my employees.

12. New ideas get implemented successfully and on time.

13. I know the value of my company and have an exit strategy in place.

14. Our technology is up to date and all software is properly licensed.

15. I know exactly how to motivate and get the most out of my key people.

16. I'm having fun in my job.

17. I know my greatest priority over the next few months and the next year.

18. We have both a sales and marketing plan in place and follow them.

19. We regularly get outside input and use that input.

20. My company, its culture, and my employees are poised for growth.

21. Our management team works synergistically for the company's growth, with little need to defend their turf and ideas.

22. Our customers share our perception of our products and services.

Appendix D

Sample Time Line to Closing

Done	Action	Target Date
____	Preliminary Committal Letter from Bank	
____	LOI signed	
____	All financial information for bank, from seller	
____	Buyer applies for life insurance	
____	Package to bank(s)	
____	Buyer-seller initial due diligence meeting	
____	Bank package to credit department	
____	Due diligence - next milestone	
____	Legal documents - drafting started	
____	Meet landlord - discuss lease	
____	Bank review completed	
____	Financial due diligence approved	
____	Buyer calls customers as "references" or similar	
____	Bank request for tax returns (form 4506, seller signs)	
____	Bank orders business valuation and home appraisal	
____	Landlord wavier draft-language (from bank)	
____	Escrow agent alerted	
____	Asset allocation from CPAs	
____	Final draft of legal documents	
____	Promissory note	
____	Security agreement to band	
____	Lease - tentative approval by both parties	
____	Life insurance approved	
____	Business valuation completed	
____	Home appraisal completed	
____	Bank documents ready	
____	All docs ready for signing	
____	Buyer meets employees	
____	Signing of subordination agreement by Seller	
____	Buyer's money in Escrow Account	

Diana Altchech can be reached at Diana@actconsultants.com or 206-999-6397.

Appendix E

Typical SBA loan requirements, as of the time of publishing.

BUSINESS INFO (Seller)

- Last three years of business tax returns
- Year to date (YTD) profit-and-loss statement and balance sheet
- A/R and A/P aging dated the same date as the YTD financial statements
- Inventory listing dated the same date as the interim statements
- Trailing twelve-month financial statement, on a month-to-month basis
- Work-in-progress report for each three fiscal year-ends and YTD if applicable
- Equipment listing (serial numbers should be provided for any item with an estimated value exceeding $5000)
- Bank to complete walkthrough to verify equipment

BUSINESS INFO (Buyer)

- One year of month-to-month projections for upcoming year
- Lease agreement
- Term of lease must meet or exceed term of loan, including option to extend

GUARANTOR INFO (All owners more than 20 percent)

- Management resume form (attached)
- Signed personal financial statement (dated within last forty-five days)
- Three years of personal tax returns

INSURANCE

- All collateral must be insured for replacement value
- General liability insurance
- Flood insurance on all assets in a flood zone
- Life insurance in the amount of the loan

OTHER

- Final purchase and sale agreement, inclusive of breakdown of purchase price
- Source of equity injection and supporting documentation
- Copy of seller carry-back loan (if any)
- Portion considered equity to be on full standby (no principal or interest), two years minimum
- Business valuation (third-party valuation to be ordered by the bank)
- Entity documentation

Appendix F

If your banker decides she wants an asset audit, you'll be asked to provide the auditor and buyer with the items listed below. This is usually done when there are high levels of accounts receivable and inventory included in the deal (and the bank's collateral).

Accounts receivable (for all divisions, as applicable)

1. A detailed A/R aging as of two months from the most recent month closed. A sample of payments will be selected from this aging by reviewing invoices that are absent from it in comparison to the current aging.

2. Monthly cash receipts and sales journals for the last thirteen months closed.

3. A detail of credit memos issued during the most recent thirteen months closed. Depending on the results of other testing, a sample of credit memos may be picked for further testing.

4. Accounts receivable roll-forward for each of the last thirteen months closed (beginning balance + sales-collections +/-debits/credits = end balance). Details will be needed for all cash received, discounts, credit memos, gross sales, and miscellaneous credits.

5. An accounts receivable aging will be needed as of the Friday before the start of the exam or the day of the exam. A sample of invoices will be selected from this accounts receivable aging. We will need to review the original invoice, bill of lading, and purchase orders to support the invoice selected.

6. Monthly summary A/R agings for the last thirteen months closed.

7. A listing of total sales for the company's top fifteen customers for the last thirteen months.

Inventory (for all divisions, as applicable)

1. Breakdown of the inventory by location including address and dollar value. Please indicate if the location is leased or owned.

2. Breakdown of inventory by raw materials, work in progress and finished goods from each location.

3. Reconciliation of latest physical inventory report to the general ledger and to the F/S.

4. Current insurance policy/certificate that covers all locations.

5. Monthly perpetual inventory report for the most recent thirteen months closed, which details inventory on hand by SKU by both quantity and amount. Please ensure it denotes raw materials, WIP, and finished goods.

6. Usage or sales history reports showing period's usage/sales for all SKUs, if available, over the last thirteen months.

7. Perpetual report as of the Friday before the start of the exam or the day before the exam.

8. A report or schedule showing the cost of completing the WIP inventory if applicable.

9. Test counts will be performed at the more populated locations.

10. Cost test will be performed on a selected sample of the inventory.

11. A summary of adjustments made to inventory as a result of the three most recent test counts performed by internal personnel.

Accounts Payable

1. A/P agings for the last thirteen months closed.

2. Breakdown of accruals for the last month closed.

3. A/P reconciliation from the A/P aging, to the general ledger and to the financial statement for the most current month closed.

4. Check registers for the most recent three months so that a sample of disbursements can be selected. Copies of the check or wire form, a copy of the vendor invoice, proof that the payment cleared on the bank statement, and other documentation supporting the disbursement will be received for reasonableness.

5. A listing of the top fifteen vendors by total purchases for the past thirteen months.

Other

1. Balance sheet and P&L statements for the most recent three months closed.

2. Financial statements for the three most recent fiscal year-ends.

3. Taxes—federal and state payroll taxes, federal and state income taxes, real estate taxes, personal property, and property taxes. Proof of payment is needed for the most recent month, quarter of year paid.

4. Latest three months of bank reconciliations, bank statements, and canceled checks for all cash accounts.

5. Month-end and weekly collateral report for the past thirteen months if applicable.

6. General ledger—detail by month for the most recent thirteen months closed. Note: If general ledger is voluminous, please print the accounts receivable trade account; other accounts may be requested later. A summary trial balance will be required.

7. A copy of the insurance certificates supporting current insurance coverage. Proof of payment for the most recent period will also need to be reviewed.

Appendix G

Your buyer must handle the following:

Government

- Federal and state registrations including EIN number and possibly S corp registration
- County and city registrations, permits, and licenses
- Picking a company name and registering it
- Hazardous materials
- Confirm seller's existing corporation or LLC existence
- Registered agents' address
- All tax forms: Workers' Comp, excise, sales, unemployment, personal property, etc.
- If asset purchase, dissolve your entity and/or have you relinquish trade name to buyer

Nongovernment

- Bank—deposits, credit card processing, lines of credit, etc.
- Utilities—phone, electric, FedEx, UPS, USPS, etc.
- Maintenance—cleaning, equipment service, etc.
- Computers, Internet, website—buyer must get all passwords, change registrations, etc.

- Copyrights, trademarks, and other intellectual property—including trade name registration
- Insurance—property, liability, vehicle, life (bank may require), health, disability, etc.
- New business cards, stationery, labels, packaging, etc.
- Leases including property, copiers, postage meters, etc.
- Employment agreements/noncompete agreements, W-9s, and W-4s
- Contracts with vendors, customers, Yellow Pages, trade publications, etc.
- Vendor and customer lists including *all* contact information
- Change vehicle registrations
- Vendor list—must they apply for credit in advance?
- Closing reports, liens, taxes due, etc.
- Prorated expenses and revenues, including accounting for customer deposits for future work and the cash needed to fulfill such work
- Life insurance—this is a timely issue. The bank will probably require it. It takes six to eight weeks to get a policy issued so your buyer must start early.

Appendix H

The following is a list of schedules that are typically included in an asset purchase agreement or requested by a buyer in connection with disclosures required from the seller in an asset purchase agreement.

Greg Russell with PRK Law in Bellevue, WA has provided this. Greg is at 425-462-4700 and grussell@prklaw.com.

Ref.	Reference #	Title
1.	**Schedule 1.1**	Acquired Assets - lists of specific tangible assets to be included in the sale, usually including accounts receivable, inventory and equipment as of the closing
2.	**Schedule 1.2**	Excluded Assets - list of assets to be excluded from the sale, such as personal vehicles or other assets unrelated to the business being purchased but which have been included over time on the Seller's balance sheet
3.	**Schedule 1.3**	Assumed Liabilities – list of business liabilities that the Buyer will assume at closing
4.	**Schedule 1.4**	Retained Liabilities – list of specific liabilities of the business that Seller will retain and pay at or after closing
5.	**Schedule 1.5**	Purchase Price Allocation – allocation of transaction consideration among different tax and asset classes
6.	**Schedule 1.6**	Jurisdictions/Qualifications/Permits – list of Seller's jurisdiction where formed, and states or other jurisdictions where Seller is required to be registered and qualified to do business, and other permits required by the business
7.	**Schedule 1.7**	Seller Equity – description of the authorized and outstanding equity of the Seller, any equity option plans or rights to acquire Seller equity
8.	**Schedule 1.8**	Liens or Encumbrances – list of all existing liens or encumbrances on Acquired Assets
9.	**Schedule 1.9**	Notices, Consents or Approvals – list of all notices, consents or approvals required to be obtained from a governmental entity or third person in connection with the sale, including consents needed for the assignment of any material contracts from the Seller to the Buyer.
10.	**Schedule 1.10**	Financial Statements – attach financial statements (balance sheet, income statement, statements of cash flow) for specified number of prior years, and the portion of the current year prior to closing of the sale.
11.	**Schedule 1.11**	Undisclosed Liabilities – list of any liabilities that are not reflected or reserved for on the Seller's balance sheet, or current liabilities that were not incurred in the ordinary course of Seller's business
12.	**Schedule 1.12**	Absence of Changes – describe any material adverse changes to the Seller or the business since the last audited financial statement
13.	**Schedule 1.13**	Legal Compliance – describe any situations where Seller or the business is not in compliance with any federal, state or local statutes or regulations
14.	**Schedule 1.14**	Employees – list detailed information about all employees, including copies of any employment or compensation agreements, or summaries of any verbal agreements; employee census, current compensation and increases in compensation in

About the Author

John Martinka is known as The Escape Artist™ because of the work he does in three areas:

1. Creating large exits for small businesses so the owner can exit the business with style, grace, and more money

2. Accelerating businesses so they escape their plateau, dramatically increasing the value of companies

3. Helping executives escape the corporate world by buying the right business the right way

John has twenty years of business experience as an intermediary, was a cofounder of "Partner" On-Call Network, and has helped over one hundred clients successfully navigate the treacherous waters of buy-sell transactions. He was awarded "Board Approval" in business acquisitions and sales by the Society for Advancement of Consulting℠ LLC.

John works with numerous nonprofits and twice was a Rotary Club president. In 2005 he started a Rotary project in conjunction with the Newport High School (Bellevue, WA) Cisco Networking Academy to install computer labs in schools. As of this publishing, about three thousand computers have been donated and installed in Slovakia, Turkey, and Antigua and Barbuda, with the students doing most of the on-site work. Our team gone to Antigua seven times and have also distributed nine thousand dictionaries to third-grade students, provided and installed a video teleconferencing system between Antigua and Barbuda, and taught computer maintenance classes. John's wife, Jan, set up sewing centers to teach ladies living in a high-poverty area the skill of sewing, which they use to make their family clothes, school uniforms, and items they can sell.

Find out more about John and the services he offers by going to www.martinkaconsulting.com. You can reach him at john@johnmartinka.com or 425-576-1814.

Index

Made in the USA
San Bernardino, CA
17 March 2015